RUNNING WITH PAYNE

A Step-by-Step Journey Down Route 66 & Beyond

RANDY ELLIS

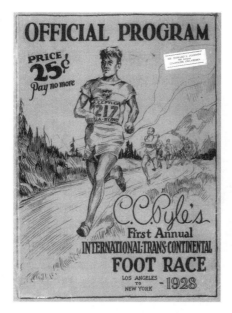

About the cover: The illustration on the front cover is from the original 1928 "First Annual International Trans-Continental Foot Race" program, pictured at left. The program was generously provided for this use by the Museum of Pioneer History in Chandler, Oklahoma; reprinted with permission.

ISBN 1-58597-313-0

Library of Congress Control Number: 2004117917

A division of Squire Publishers, Inc.
4500 College Blvd.
Leawood, KS 66211
1/888/888/7696
www.leatherspublishing.com

PREFACE

THE THOUGHT OF reliving history captures the imagination of many people as evidenced by periodic reenactments of historical events such as the Civil War. The popularity of antiques, museums, old cars and oldies music all point to the fact that we enjoy experiencing a part of the past.

As you read this book, you will share in my experiences of reliving a fascinating piece of history; a reliving that was as real and life-like as any reenactment could possibly be. This particular event in history occurred in 1928, but is now mostly forgotten. However, at the time the event took place, it captivated the attention of many people across the United States and around the world.

In 1928, in order to commemorate the completion of the new transcontinental two-lane Route 66 highway, a running race across the United States was organized and completed. Yes, that's right — a running race across the width of the entire country, incorporating the then new Route 66. The race attracted the best long-distance runners from around the world and was widely followed through newspaper articles and radio broadcasts.

A central figure in the race was a young Cherokee Indian named Andy Payne, who grew up in a small town not far from my hometown of Sapulpa, Oklahoma. As I learned more and more about Andy Payne and this historical event, I was smitten with the dream of reliving the race.

Seventy years after this race, I undertook my dream of attempting to run across the United States, from the Pacific Ocean to the Atlantic Ocean. This book parallels and contrasts my dream run with that transcontinental race and the run of Andy Payne, hence the title *Running with Payne*.

I hope you will enjoy this light-hearted account of both my dream and a fascinating piece of history. Those who know me know that I enjoy humor. At the beginning of each of the 78 days is a short title in quotes. Your mission, if you choose to accept it, is to look for the meaning or humor in the title as you read that day's account. For an additional challenge, be on the lookout for an acronym that was included in the 78-day journal, using the first letter of each day. If you don't find it, additional clues will be disclosed at the end. No peeking!

I hope the experiences shared in this book will encourage you for the difficult challenges and undertakings in your life. Many of you reading this have had moments of despair when the journey or task ahead is more than you can comprehend. Running across the country is child's play compared to the real life situations that people face on a daily basis.

For example, my friend Dale Hemphill has battled ALS/Lou Gehrig's disease for six years. He has tremendous faith, courage, and devotion to his family. Though every day is a struggle for Dale and his wife, Denise, Dale said he has never despaired because of his faith in God. Both Denise and her mother, Joann, said they have never heard him complain. Observing Dale's daily perseverance is truly a source of encouragement to me.

Similar to the manner in which Dale encourages me, my hope and prayer is that this book will provide encouragement in whatever challenge you face in life. Most importantly, I hope this book will glorify God, our Creator.

ACKNOWLEDGMENTS

EVERY TIME I think about my run across the country, I think of the many people who provided support, prayer and encouragement. I am truly humbled before God as I think of all the help that was given to me.

I am grateful for each of the 611 e-mails that were sent to me during the run. The messages of encouragement came from family, friends, and "new" friends – numerous people whom I have never met. Messages came, not only from many different states, but also from Australia, Austria, Pakistan, Kazakstan, England, and Canada.

While writing this book, I printed and read (and re-read) every one of the 611 messages. Though it has now been nearly seven years since the run, the gracious acts of kindness are more meaningful than ever. In an effort to thank each one, I've included every name from whom I received an e-mail in Appendix III at the back of the book.

The encouragement I received from many friends was overwhelming, both at the send-off celebration and at the reception when running through my hometown of Sapulpa, Oklahoma. I wish I could list every name here, as well as give a hearty thank-you handshake and hug.

I also want to thank the prayer warriors who supported me behind the scenes. Several different people, also shown in Appendix III, had volunteered to take certain days of my run and commit to pray for me particularly on those days. I still have the calendar they signed; reading through the names and dates always brings a spirit of thanksgiving for those who provided special support in this way.

Part of my extended family includes good friends whom I worked with at my former employer, Parker Drilling Company. My fellow employees already realized I was crazy, so the thought of me running across the country probably didn't surprise them as much as it did others. I appreciate the Parker friendship and particularly the help of Roger Fox, who coordinated the providing of a laptop computer and my own website so that I could stay in contact with everyone.

My fellow members at Sapulpa Bible Church were a continual source of encouragement and prayer. David Pritz kept the congregation informed with maps and updates and provided much help and support. Thanks also goes to my brother, Wayne Ellis, nephew, Ryan Ellis, and good friends, Eric Freeman and Kevin King, who spent a few days on the road as my crew. Also, thanks goes to my Uncle Marvin Ellis, who wrote and sang the culminating song, "Run, Randy, Run." In addition, I appreciate the encouragement and editing work of Lynna Blackwell and Eric and Laurie Freeman.

One critical element required for a major undertaking is family support. Spending 11 weeks running across the country does tend to interrupt the normal family schedule. Not being able to attend all the concerts, games, and activities of my children was one of the most difficult aspects of the run. However, my children, Heather, Justin and Nicole, could not have been any more supportive. They pitched in and helped their mother and made sure all the necessary things were accomplished. Heather and Justin also spent a few days on the road providing crew services. I will always be grateful for my children's love and support.

I would never have accomplished the dream without the loving support of my wife, Marcy. There were times before the run had started when I wanted to throw in the towel, but she kept me committed to the dream. The adventure was certainly a much bigger sacrifice on her part than on mine. No one could ever hope for a more supportive, loving spouse. It's been a wonderful 30 years together.

However, it was my parents, Calvin and Hazel Ellis, who made the biggest sacrifice. They basically gave up 12 weeks of their lives in order to wait on me hand and foot. The sacrificial love of my parents in laying aside their life for their children is an example of Jesus' love and laying down His life for His people.

Dad was with me for all but six days during that time, serving as chief navigator, chief doctor and overall chief coordinator. Mom was with me over half the days, being chief cook, chief clothing coordinator and chief prayer warrior. They were an integral part of the dream; no words can ever convey my appreciation for them!

TABLE OF CONTENTS

1

WHY? WHY? WHY?

"OUT OF THE mouths of babes," the saying goes. Sure enough, it took a five-year-old to succinctly summarize the absurdity of attempting to run across the United States from the Pacific to the Atlantic Ocean. I was just over halfway through my cross-country journey and lost in my thoughts as I ran on Route 66 through the outskirts of Chandler, Oklahoma. Two young boys were yelling and playing in the fenced front yard of a small house as I passed by on the road. When they noticed me, the two boys ran to the fence and peered through the bushes to see this strange sight going by their house.

I greeted them, "Hi, guys."

The blonde-headed boy asked, "Whatcha doin'?"

Wondering how much they would comprehend, I stopped running and answered, "I'm running across the country."

He replied, "Where you goin'?"

Thinking he could never grasp the enormity of the task, I said, "I'm running to the Atlantic Ocean."

His curiosity aroused, he asked, "How far is that?"

Watching how he would react, I matter-of-factly replied "Well, it's over one thousand miles. I started running in California and I have over one thousand miles left."

There was a momentary pause as he thought through what he had just heard. Then his blond eyebrows suddenly arched upwards, and with a proud look he declared, "Buy you a car."

There! He had single-handedly, at the young age of five, solved the dilemma that he sensed I was facing. A car would be much easier and faster, wouldn't it? No rational person would be running across the country when there was such an easy alternative available, would he? And, in today's world, if you want something, you just go out and buy it. Yes, even a five-year-old knew there was no logical reason why a person would run across the country.

Why? It was the question heard from everyone. It came in many forms and was posed in various ways, but the basic question was always the same: Why? Why would you want to do that? Was someone chasing you? Are you running a race? Are you getting paid for it? Are you doing it for a worthy cause (as though attempting to accomplish one's own dreams is not a worthy cause)? Why? Why? Why?

One's own personal dreams are not always easy to explain to others. The old saying, "One man's trash is another man's treasure," may have some application to dreams also. Our individual dreams often hold no charm or charisma to other people. Yet, on the other hand, one person's dream may inspire others.

Shortly after I had started my run, Roger Fox had a unique perspective when he e-mailed the following, "Randy, people may question why you do such a thing, but I am sure all respond with the same thought pattern. When we question, the inevitable answer is because it is important to him. Which followed with the introspective questioning of what is important to me and am I doing it? In your extraordinary effort, you cause others to question what is important to them, with the net result of people being bettered by what you are doing. Thanks for stretching all of us."

When I read about or watch a documentary about climbers ascending Mount Everest, I admit I ask the "why" question. Why would they dream and aspire to do that? Although I wonder why, I'm always intrigued and inspired by their endeavors. In a like manner, I have hoped that accomplishing my dream would inspire others to turn their own desires into reality.

Regardless, I always dreaded the "why" question. I tried to explain about it being a long-time dream of mine, but the answer never seemed to satisfy. I could sense that the questioner was left thinking there must be more to the story. Or, if they weren't thinking that, they were thinking there must be less. Less mental capacity on my part, that is. Although there weren't many, there were a few who came right out and questioned the mental capacity of someone who would attempt such an undertaking.

One of the notable mental-capacity questioners came from a surprising source, the greeter at the front door of First Baptist Church in Grants, New Mexico. It was my custom on Sunday mornings to run for three hours or so in the early morning and then clean up to attend church services.

When entering a new church, we were generally recognized as visitors and often asked if we were from out of town and why we were in the area. On this particular Sunday morning, my dad chose to tell the elderly gentleman at the door greeting incoming people that I was running across the United States. With a puzzled look, the gentleman looked at me and asked, "Has he been in the sun too long?" Of course, most people are not that direct, but I'm sure he merely expressed what many people thought when they asked the "why" question.

During the worship service that Sunday morning, the pastor's sermon topic was the beautiful gift of the voice that God has given us and how it can used for His glory. Don't get me wrong, my feelings weren't hurt from the "out in the sun" comment; however, I was hoping the door greeter was taking note of the sermon. It didn't bother me that he would question my sanity and make that comment without knowing me. Really, it didn't matter at all. Well, okay, maybe just a little.

Yes, the "why" question was posed by all sorts of different people, in an assortment of different manners. However, the most forceful and disturbing "why" question was asked by — guess who? — me, myself. The "why" question had occasionally entered my mind but was always easily dismissed by the excitement of planning the adventure. However, this time the "why" of the whole adventure descended upon me suddenly and with great force. It was as though every "why" question was rolled into one big, "You are crazy! Why are you doing this?"

On the very first day of running across the country, I had run three miles in a dream-like state of euphoria when suddenly the reality of the situation overwhelmed me as I thought, "I have gone three miles and I have about three thousand miles to go. THREE THOUSAND miles to go! On foot! Three down, and THREE THOUSAND to go! On foot! What in the world am I doing? What have I gotten myself into now? I am unemployed — having left a good job to train for and to attempt this run. What sane person would ever do this? Why? WHY?"

For the first time, doubt and fear were beginning to checkmate the thrill of attempting the dream. Often there had been some anxiety, but that was to be expected when taking on a challenging task. I had often drawn inspiration from others' accomplishments to tame my anxieties. But now, after only three miles, surrounded by strangers walking the streets of Santa Monica, I felt anxiety quietly turning into despair.

"Despair!" That's a word that accompanies cancer, divorce, or death of loved ones, not an exciting adventure. However, thinking about the enormous task I had set for myself had led to anxiety, discouragement, and now, despair. After a few moments, I turned to my always-present source of hope and comfort, and prayed, "God, I now realize more than ever before, I am in Your hands. Only by Your strength and blessings will I be able to accomplish my dream." I thought of His words, *"My grace is sufficient for you, for My strength is made perfect in weakness"* (II Corinthians 12:9).

The song, "One Day at a Time," came to me and reminded me to not think of the whole journey. It was too overwhelming. "God will provide strength for today," I thought. "Just take it one step at a time – one day at a time."

The joy of the journey quickly returned, and I rarely thought again of all that lay ahead. God's words spoke to my heart again, *"But seek first the kingdom of God and His righteousness and all these things shall be added to you. Therefore, do not worry about tomorrow, tomorrow will worry about its own things. Sufficient for the day is its own trouble"* (Matthew 6:33-34).

Through the years I had often been inspired by the adventures of others; however, inspiration had never before been replaced with complete captivation. Then I read one story which captured my imagination.

In 1992 I entered the Andy Payne Memorial Marathon Race in Oklahoma City. Inside the race packet was a small pamphlet giving information about the race's namesake.

After driving home from the race, I read the pamphlet and was immediately intrigued by the story. I had previously run several ultra-marathon races of 50 and 100 miles. Those distances seemed long, but the pamphlet told about the ultimate long distance race: a race in 1928 from Los Angeles to New York.

I called the race director and asked for more information about this cross-country race and the memorial honoree, Andy Payne. After reading two books about the race, plus old newspaper accounts at the library, I was an Andy Payne fan. The dream had begun.

Andy Payne, a Cherokee Indian, graduated from high school in Foyil, Oklahoma, in May 1927. Though he grew up on a farm, he did not like farm work or, ironically, riding horses. He often ran the five miles to school rather than ride horses like his broth-

5

ers and sisters. He developed into a good runner and was one of the top local milers in high school.

Upon graduation, he hitchhiked to California to find a job and make his own way. It was in Los Angeles that he saw the advertisement that caught his attention and captured his imagination. His dream had begun.

Per the advertisement, on March 4, 1928, the Transcontinental Footrace would start in Los Angeles and finish weeks later in New York, encompassing the length (Los Angeles to Chicago) of the newly developed Route 66. Total prize money being offered was $48,000, with $25,000 going to the winner of the race. The purpose of the race was to bring publicity to the new super transcontinental highway. (It's hard for us today to imagine the excitement over a two-lane, no-shoulder highway that wasn't even completely paved at that time.)

Andy began to dream what he could do with $25,000. (The purchasing power of that amount of money in his day would likely exceed $600,000 in today's dollars.) First of all, he could help pay off his dad's heavily mortgaged farm. Secondly, a young math/Spanish teacher had begun to teach at Foyil High School during Andy's senior year. Andy soon had a schoolboy crush. She was beautiful and only one year older than he was. If he could win the top prize, he could catch her attention and, just maybe, win her heart.

The race required a deposit of $100 as an entry fee, an amount of money that Payne did not have. He hitchhiked back to his hometown in Oklahoma in an effort to borrow the money. He and his dad found no willing sponsor, so they eventually borrowed the required sum of money. Payne hitchhiked back to the Los Angeles area and began training in earnest for the race in January 1928.

In late February, the best long-distance runners in the world assembled for the race, including South Africa's Arthur Newton, who held all the long-distance world records. Runners came from Europe, Asia, South America, all over the United States, and included a few of the legendary Tahumara Indians from Mexico.

On March 4, 1928, on the muddy horse track of Ascott Speedway, the gun was fired and 199 runners began the great Transcontinental Footrace across Route 66, which became known as the "Bunion Derby." It was a stage race, much like today's Tour de France bicycle race. There was a specific starting point and ending point each day. Wherever one day ended was where the runners would resume the next morning. Daily segments would generally range from 30 to 50 miles, with an average of about 40 miles per day. A runner had to complete each daily segment or be disqualified. The runner with the lowest cumulative time at the completion of all the daily stages would be the winner.

There was a magical thrill to the story, and it captured my imagination. I could envision the excitement and imagine what it would have been like to be a part of the Bunion Derby entourage. The dream of recreating the race and running across the country like they did began forming in my mind. Soon, the dream had captivated me.

Part of the thrill of my run was running on the same roads and through the same places that Andy Payne and the Bunion Derby runners had run, hence the title of the book. As I ran, I often dreamed about what it was like in 1928 as they raced across America. My imagination was so strong at times, I felt as though I was *Running With Payne.*

I told the Andy Payne story so many times to so many people, my family became very tired of hearing it. As I would start to tell my often-recited story to someone, one of my kids would say, "Andy Payne again!" Of course, they may have overdosed on Andy Payne due to my questioning them every time we drove on an old section of Route 66, "Do you know who ran on this road?" The kids would answer in bored unison, "Andy Payne." In my mind, I knew they were just feigning boredom with the story. It was too exciting for them not to want to be reminded of it time after time — or so I had convinced myself.

My dear wife, Marcy, now had to endure not only hearing the Andy Payne stories, but also hearing my dream of attempting the run myself. It was obvious it would take a tremendous commitment of time, money, and family involvement to pull it off. We saved and dreamed, or at least, I dreamed. After several years of my stories and dreaming of doing the run, Marcy finally said, "If you're going to do it, now is the time." Yes! I had finally worn her down. Um, what I mean is that I had solicited and obtained her approval.

The next step was to talk to my parents, knowing we would need much support and help from them. After the initial shock, my father, Calvin, caught the dream and said, "I will help you in whatever way I can."

At the time, I was the Controller at Parker Drilling Company. I knew there was no way to take off the five to six months it would take to train for, and then accomplish, the run. The dream began to turn into reality in August 1997, when I told the company that I would be leaving at the end of January. I was then committed for sure. There would be no turning back now, or, at least, no turning back without suffering a high degree of disappointment and embarrassment.

ANDREW PAYNE
Claremore, Okla.

An athletic product of Oklahoma high school. Ran in the State Championships at Norman. Has trained faithfully on Oklahoma roads for many months and is a strong lad and a natural runner who depends on his youth and strength.

The actual bio of Andy Payne from the official program of the 1928 Bunion Derby.

2

RUNNING A MILE IN
SOMEONE ELSE'S SHOES

HAVING MADE THE commitment, the first thing I wanted to accomplish was to drive to Los Angeles and plot my route back to Oklahoma. Over one-half of the run would be on historic Route 66, but in many places the old, historic Route 66 was either fenced off in private land or buried underneath the modern transcontinental highway, Interstate 40. It was in those areas where I would have to find alternative routes.

In October 1997, I rented a car with unlimited mileage (imagine their surprise when it was returned five days later with an added 3,500 miles) and took off by myself from my hometown of Sapulpa, Oklahoma, early on a Wednesday morning, maps and notebooks in hand — or on the front seat. It was very exciting to drive to California and envision the dream starting to come to fruition. That is, it was exciting right up until the time I reached the nightmare known as Los Angeles. I was overwhelmed as I negotiated many miles of traffic, hotels, fast food restaurants, and everything you could imagine on the old Route 66 from San Bernardino through a myriad of Los Angeles suburbs to Santa Monica.

The enthusiasm had waned as I sat in my Santa Monica hotel room that Thursday night. I could not imagine running the first 70 miles through constant traffic and masses of people. I had planned to start my run at the end (or is it the beginning?) of Route 66 at the Santa Monica Pier and run as much of Route 66 as possible. I glumly opened my map in the hotel room and wondered if there could be a better way to escape Los Angeles traffic. As I studied the map, I saw a possible answer: if I would sacrifice by not running on Route 66 for several miles, I could head directly north out of Santa Monica and escape the Los Angeles area much quicker. I determined to drive that way the next morning and check it out.

Early on Friday morning, I drove to the Santa Monica Pier and imagined what it would be like in five months when I started the run, if that time would ever arrive. After exploring the expected starting area around the pier for less than one hour, it was back into the car and heading north out of the Los Angeles area, trying my new route. As I drove along highways that largely avoided bumper-to-bumper traffic and masses of humanity, I thought, "Yes, this is the way to run. I will get out of the Los Angeles metro area as quickly as possible, even if it means running less of the Bunion Derby Route 66 course."

On the long drive back to Oklahoma, the fatigue of driving 3,500 miles in four days had sapped my enthusiasm and made me realize that this would indeed be a long, long run and a difficult endeavor. Covering the 1,500 miles from Los Angeles to my hometown of Sapulpa, Oklahoma would barely reach halfway to the east coast. I was discouraged as I arrived at home and mentioned to Marcy, "I'm not sure if I should do this or not."

Marcy, ever the encourager, said, "You've committed; you have to do it, and you will do it." We never questioned the decision from that point, at least not until the previously mentioned despair overtook me three miles into the run.

I left my job in January and started my new non-paying job:

training for several hours a day. I had been training for long distances for several years, but now was the time to really step up the effort. Many days I ran and walked for 20 or more miles. Sometimes I would run most of the miles; other days I would walk up to 18 miles at a time. The Lord was gracious and protected me from injury. An injury would have been the one thing that could turn the dream into a deflated balloon.

Several weeks before the projected starting date, Dad and I began scouring the area for an older used motor home that could make it across the country. We eventually found and purchased one that would be our "home away from home." At the time, I probably had more confidence in the motor home making it across the country than I had in myself. Actually, the motor home had the more difficult task, wouldn't it? It would have to make it across the country twice: out to the west coast, across the country, and back from the east coast. I only had to make it across the country once. You don't really believe that story about Forrest Gump making it across the country, only to turn around and start again, do you?

Another plan that I had formulated in my mind was to raise contributions for a local charity. I arranged to be present at one of the directors' meetings for Community Care, a charitable organization based in my hometown that provides food and clothing to the needy in our area. My mom had been instrumental in creating Community Care. Mary Walters, long-time manager, continues to do a wonderful job of meeting needs in the community.

As I laid out my plan of running across the country, they were just as startled as everyone else that someone would actually want to do that. I'm sure I was asked why. The directors seemed excited that I was offering to raise pledges of so much per mile that would be donated to Community Care. Sandy Howard was particularly helpful in making plans and designing a commemorative tee shirt that could be sold to raise funds for the organization.

Often I have been asked if I had any sponsors. I only attempted to obtain sponsorship one time. Knowing I would need several pairs of running shoes, I wrote a letter to Alberto Salazar, renowned marathon runner and officer of Nike. Not surprisingly, I received a nice, but not interested, note back – probably from a low-level assistant. I'm sure I was too small a fish to even consider helping, especially considering the millions paid to Michael. I figured it was their missed opportunity. However, I did keep the note to provide a little extra incentive.

I picked Saturday, March 28, as the anticipated starting date. A Saturday start would give me two weekend days to get away from Los Angeles before the Monday morning work traffic. The late March starting date would allow me to avoid the winter weather, yet finish before the worst of the summer heat. The last several weeks before the run went by quickly and it was soon time to head west.

On the morning of Wednesday, March 25, the Sapulpa community had a celebration in honor of its centennial at Martha's Corner, a small park in downtown Sapulpa. Oklahoma's first lady, Kathy Keating, was the community's special guest. I was honored to be a part of the program, as the community connected my send-off with the celebration. I was given a Sapulpa Centennial flag, which would resurface later in the journey. One of the Tulsa television stations, along with radio station KRMG, were both present doing interviews. It was an honor to be interviewed by my all-time favorite television newscaster, Jerry Webber, who has since passed away from cancer.

Having family and many friends there made for an emotional and exciting time. My daughter Heather, who was attending the University of Arkansas, surprised me by missing classes and driving two hours from Fayetteville, Arkansas. In order to obtain an excused absence, she had approached one of her professors and told him why she would be missing class. After he heard about her father's send-off to run across the country, he said, "If that is a made-up story, it's the best one I have ever heard." The professor's comment sort of goes along with the "why" question, doesn't it?

After the ceremony and the interviews, family and friends gathered in a circle and held hands while Pastor John Nelson led everyone in prayer. At about noon, it was time for Dad, Mom, Marcy, and myself to load up in the motor home and head to the West Coast. It was a thrill and an honor to have so many people say good-bye as we exited downtown Sapulpa, having no idea what the next three months held in store.

We arrived in the Los Angeles area Friday afternoon and met our friend, Mike Fanning, a seminary student and head of security at the Master's College in the Los Angeles suburb of Valencia. He graciously allowed us to use the college facilities and to hook up electricity for the motor home. This would be our camping spot the night before the start and the night after the first day. Mike's assistance in getting us off to a good start was much appreciated.

Mike's parents had become members of our home church, Sapulpa Bible Church, after he, his wife Karen, and their three children had moved to California to go to seminary. As God would work it out, Mike would later become our pastor at Sapulpa Bible Church after he finished seminary.

As I lay in bed on Friday night, I thought of all the years I had dreamed of this, all the training miles in preparation, all the plans, all the speaking engagements, and the number of times I had shared the Bunion Derby story. Now, the start was less than nine hours away. It was just like our everyday life: we make many plans, but we still enter the unknown every day. *"A man's heart plans his way, but the Lord directs his steps"* (Proverbs 16:9).

It was very exciting to wake up on Saturday morning and realize that the big day had finally arrived. The one specific day

I had dreamed about for several years was here. I repeatedly had to convince myself that this was no longer a dream, this was actually happening! Mom said numerous times, "I can't believe we're really doing this." During the run I would get e-mails from friends who would say, "I can't believe you're doing this." As a matter of fact, I often thought, "I can't believe I am doing this."

As we drove the 20 miles from the Master's College to Santa Monica Beach, raindrops began to pepper the windshield of the motor home. Wait just a minute here! Starting in the rain was not what I envisioned when I had dreamed about the first morning.

Thankfully, the rain stopped before we arrived at the beach. Soon, the moment which I had dreamed and prayed about, planned and trained for, had come. I knew many friends were thinking of and praying for me that morning. A few people had said they had friends or relatives in the Los Angeles area who might show up for the 7 a.m. start by the Santa Monica Pier. However, it was only Dad, Mom, Marcy, and I who gathered on the beach that surreal morning.

I had a desire to not only capture the moment with pictures but also, for some strange reason, to capture some of the Pacific Ocean water. I thought that if I should actually reach the Atlantic Ocean, I would pour some of the Pacific into the Atlantic. I didn't anticipate some chemical, foaming reaction. It just seemed like the symbolic thing to do. I filled two empty plastic milk jugs with Pacific Ocean water to be stashed away in the motor home for the cross-country trip. We took a few pictures on the beach and prayed to God for His protection and strength to face whatever lay ahead. I had no idea what to expect. I had run many long-distance races, but I was getting ready to enter foreign territory. The task ahead seemed huge, and I sensed it was only by God's enabling blessings that I would be able to accomplish the goal.

Although I had purchased, and lightly broken in, six new

pairs of Asics running shoes (could have been Nikes had they been interested), I started the run in the oldest, most faded and most worn-out Adidas running shoes imaginable. The blue canvas had faded to a greenish color and was torn in places. The rubber soles were now the consistency of petrified wood. The shoes offered little protection, and I was sure they wouldn't hold together for very long. I would have been embarrassed to give these shoes to the Goodwill store. Besides all that, they were about one and one-half sizes too small. However, it was an honor for me to start in these shoes, and it would be an honor if I could finish in them. These were not my shoes. I was wearing someone else's shoes, shoes that I could never fill.

My grandfather, Harvey Ellis, had died at the age of 90 about a year before I started my run. During the last years of his life, he always wore those old shoes. Upon his death, and since I was already planning my run, I requested that I be given those shoes.

Running across the country was going to take physical endurance. However, my Grandpa Ellis was a real man of endurance, not running, but real life endurance. He had been married 60 years to his wife Letha before she died. Grandpa worked at Liberty Glass Plant in Sapulpa, Oklahoma, for 48 years, from 17 years of age until his retirement at 65. Working at a glass plant was extremely hot and difficult work. He raised five sons, a feat in itself, and pastored a small local church for nearly 40 years.

Starting in his shoes, shoes that were tight, yet which I couldn't fill, was my tribute to a man of real endurance. I later donned one of my father's special running shirts as a tribute to him, someone who had always been a great encouragement and who would be the greatest help on my run.

Randy by the Santa Monica Pier: Pacific Ocean water in the jug, grandfather's shoes on the feet, ready to begin the run!

First steps out of the Pacific Ocean — heading east!

3

LET THE RUN BEGIN

Day 1, March 28.
Santa Monica Beach, CA to Santa Clarita, CA — 35.0 miles.
"Pier Pressure"

"GOSH," I KEPT thinking, "Is this really happening?" All the years of reading about the Bunion Derby and dreaming and planning my own cross-country run, and now the start was here. The excitement and rush of adrenaline are impossible to describe. I waded out into knee-deep water before I started the run. To me, an ocean-to-ocean run meant out of one ocean into the other. Without fanfare, I ran out of the water, across the beach, and down the parking lot to the motor home. First order of business was to change out of Grandpa's tight and fragile shoes. We stashed them away in the motor home, dreaming of, and hoping for, the day I would put them on again and run into the Atlantic Ocean.

After changing shoes, I ran down the parking lot and climbed the steps leading up to the Santa Monica Pier. I felt like I was floating along, scarcely touching the pier as I headed for the streets of Santa Monica. Excitement is best experienced when it is shared with others, wouldn't you agree? That's what I thought. As I ran past people, I would smile and say cheerfully, "Good morning." After all, this was way beyond a good morning, this was a grand and most glorious morning. I soon realized that this morning was apparently grand and glorious only to me. Sharing with strangers is not a good idea in Los Angeles. My attempt to share and spread my enthusiasm was met with cold stares. "Who is this goofball, anyway?"

I realized that if they only knew what this tall, strange-looking guy was embarking upon, they would question the sanity of this guy all the more. In the beginning, I felt strange and out of place running through the streets of Santa Monica. Soon, I realized that in the diverse culture of the Los Angeles area, nothing can look strange and out of place.

Amidst countless people, I blissfully ran alone in my own joyful world. It was joyful all except for the few minutes of panic at the three-mile mark as the reality of the undertaking hit me. As we tend to do during difficult undertakings in life, I prayed and asked God to give me the strength to do whatever had to be done.

Most of the first day's run was spent staying alert and negotiating traffic. After the first four miles, I turned off Santa Monica Blvd. north onto Sepulveda Blvd. Later I ran north on Balboa Street and reached Santa Clarita, where I called it a day after a total of 35 miles. During the day, my crew would go ahead six or seven miles and try to find a good parking place to wait for me. I would take a short break at each stopping point, catching up on liquids and snacking lightly. This was a new experience, or new experiment, for all of us.

One thing I sadly noticed this day was numerous shopping carts — not at the stores, but under bridges and anywhere street people would stay. It appeared that many people were pushing a shopping cart with all their possessions piled into it. Realizing the living conditions of these people made me feel blessed to have the opportunity, support, and means to be starting out on a cross-country adventure. The crowded living conditions in our motor home would seem like a vacation in spacious quarters for many of these people.

At the conclusion of the day's run, it was back to the Master's College for the night. Mike had the gym open for us to use the restrooms and showers. Boy, did that hot shower feel good! What felt even better was knowing that I had 35 miles of the Los Angeles traffic behind me.

Day 2, March 29.
Santa Clarita, CA to Palmdale, CA — 33.0 miles.
"Modern Day Hillbillies"

OFF TO AN early 6 a.m. start, I ran about 14.5 miles on the Sierra Highway before taking a break at 9 a.m. We drove the motor home about 20 miles back to Grace Community Church in northern Los Angeles. As Dad drove, I attempted to take a shower in the small cubbyhole of a shower. Bouncing around in the shower and then trying to get dressed was certainly more hazardous than the run. How would I ever explain it if the cross-country run was short-circuited by a wrenched knee suffered when falling out of shower stall in a moving motor home?

Picture a 28-foot-long older motor home with two bicycles and several lawn chairs strapped on the back, driving into a sophisticated Los Angeles suburb and pulling into the parking lot of a church that has about 7,000 people attending services on Sunday mornings. Beverly Hillbillies, I tell you! I know the people were thinking that an only slightly more modern version of the Beverly Hillbillies had just arrived. The parking lot attendants quickly waved us into an out-of-the-way parking place. I'm sure they wanted to get the motor home off the street and hidden as quickly as possible.

Undaunted, we parked where they directed and exited the

motor home as people watched. By cracky, we just went and tooked our Bibles and goed on to the high falutin' church house and just plain o' made ussins right cheer at home.

Actually, we tried to act normal as we met Mike and Karen and their children and very much enjoyed the large worship service. We were able to meet Pastor John MacArthur, a very accomplished author and teacher who has his own daily radio broadcast called "Grace to You."

Afterward, it was 20 miles of driving back to the spot where I had stopped in the morning. I ran another 19 miles in the afternoon, reaching the town of Palmdale. One of the most difficult moments of the run occurred at 4 o'clock in the afternoon when Mike and Karen picked up Marcy to take her to the airport to fly back home to take care of our children. I knew it would likely be at least five weeks before I saw her again. It was a difficult and sad good-bye, making the last part of the run on this day less exciting.

Day 3, March 30.
Palmdale, CA to Victorville, CA — 37.0 miles.
"Tendon Business"

DUDE, WHAT EVER happened to that sunny, warm southern California thing? When we awoke, we looked out the motor home window and saw ice on the puddles in the graveled parking lot where we camped for the night. A local resident told us that it had been the coldest day and night of the year for them.

Cooler weather brought no complaints from me. The temperature was very pleasant during the 37-mile run to Victorville, first on Highway 138 and then Highway 18. The view of the snow-covered mountains to the south was beautiful. I noticed a couple of snow-covered cars coming from the direction of the mountains early in the morning.

Dad had been an accomplished runner in the Tulsa area, often winning his age bracket in races. He joined me for the last five miles of the day, while Mom waited at the RV Park in Victorville, our destination for the day.

This day included constant foot doctoring, which would be our usual custom for the first couple of weeks. The bottom of one foot, as well as the Achilles tendon, became sore during the day. Every few miles Dad and I would experiment with different shoe inserts. We would put in, take out, cut holes, add, take away, put back, etc. In a few days' time, we went through a large amount of tape and shoe paraphernalia. After a few days of this, I concluded that it wasn't so much that anything actually worked, but it was simply the fact that any alteration seemed to help in that it would temporarily change the pressure points on the feet and toes.

One of the highlights of every day on the road was logging onto a laptop computer every evening and checking my website for e-mail messages. My former employer, Parker Drilling Company, had loaned me a laptop computer, a portable telephone, and the necessary equipment for dial-up connection.

Roger Fox, manager of Information Systems, was instrumental in setting up my own website where I could receive and send e-mail messages. This proved to be a tremendous source of encouragement, as I was able to communicate with family and friends, as well as with many people whom I had never met. Every evening I would post a summary of the day's run and events. Every evening, that is, that we could make a dial-up connection with the cell phone. There were several nights that we could not make a connection due to the remoteness of our location. Any night we could not access the website was disappointing due to not being able to receive encouraging e-mails.

We had gotten off to a shaky start using the website the first two days of the run, mostly due to operator error and/or ignorance. The Beverly Hillbillies never had to fool with this here computer contraptions. After a few phone calls to my brother, Craig, as well as to the Parker Drilling folks, we were educated as to what was required to make everything work. It was a joy to begin hearing from the home folks! One of the first messages that my website received was from my daughter Heather who wrote, "This is a test to see if your e-mail is up and running ... and, yes, that pun was intended."

Day 4, March 31.
Victorville, CA to Barstow, CA — 38.0 miles.
"Payneful Road"

THIS WAS AN exciting day in that I rejoined Route 66 and the Bunion Derby course when starting the morning in Victorville. I ran 38 miles from Victorville to Barstow on my fourth day, the same segment and same roads that the Bunion Derby runners did on their fourth day. Now I was truly *Running with Payne.*

On March 4, 1928, the crowds had gathered at the Ascott Speedway horse track in Los Angeles to watch the start of the Bunion Derby. The runners ran a lap and a half on the muddy track before taking off on Route 66. After a short first day of 17 miles, the race began in earnest on the second day. After three days of running, the race had reached Victorville.

I also had reached Victorville in three days, but by taking a different route out of Los Angeles. However, on this the fourth day, I felt as though I had joined and was running with the Bunion Derby runners. Often during the day and the days to come, I imagined what it was like in 1928, as the running entourage proceeded down old Route 66, just like I was doing only with much less fanfare. For the next few days, I would do nearly the same daily segments as those runners had done.

At the end of the day, I wrote on my website that Andy Payne had done this segment faster than I had. Friend Lynna Blackwell sent an e-mail saying, "You mentioned that your run from Victorsville to Barstow was a little slower than Andy Payne's. Please remember that he was half your age!" His 19 years of age to my 46 years of age might have been a slight advantage for him — but he didn't have my crew!

I was thankful that the Achilles tendon had not been a problem; however, the bruise on the bottom of one foot continued to be painful. Icing in the evenings seemed to help. This was only the start of who knows how many bags of ice we would use in the next few weeks.

After long, tiring days on the road and seeing only the faces of strangers, dialing into the website in the evening was an oasis. There were always encouraging messages from family and friends, as well as from people I had never met. The messages came from around the globe.

At the beginning of my run, I received this message: "Even though my wife and I have not met you, just want you to know that you and your family will be in our thoughts and prayers. We will check in with your page as often as possible and see how you are doing." It was from Greg and Kathy Pollard working for Parker Drilling Company in Almaty, Kazakstan.

A most encouraging and funny message came from one of my most ardent supporters, Jim Linn, senior vice-president of Parker Drilling Company. In his high school days, Jim had been an outstanding quarterback and running back at Tulsa's Nathan Hale High School. I was in grade school at that time and saw Jim play against my hometown Sapulpa High School football team. As was my custom, I would use the players from the football programs to later replay the high school games on my electric football game. I previously had told Jim that he had been a running back in my high school games on the electric football field.

Jim wrote this e-mail: "Randy, I will be praying for you daily. May you and your family be in His hedge of protection as you make your journey across this great country called America. I have the greatest respect and admiration for you. Have fun along the way. Don't look back." He added a P.S., "Did I ever score any touchdowns in electric football? I would imagine I either ran in circles or the wrong direction."

Day 5, April 1.
Barstow, CA to Newberry Springs, CA — 36.6 miles.
"Road Training"

SOLITUDE AND THE Mohave Desert were reached on this day. One of my reasons for starting the run in late March was to avoid the heat of the Mohave Desert. Boy howdy, did that plan work well! Not only was there not much heat, but I would often run in sweat pants and long sleeves through the desert and for the next four weeks. We generally had to use the motor home generator at night in order to keep warm.

It was a relief to escape the traffic and humanity of the city areas and to run across the Mohave on the seldom-used Route 66, which paralleled heavily traveled I-40. Of course, away from the crowds there was not much entertainment available. One of the enjoyable things about running in the wide-open desert spaces was being able to see the entire length of trains at one time.

On this day I passed the time by waving at the locomotive engineers as they passed on the train tracks running alongside the road. One engineer even tooted his horn after I made the motion of pulling down on my imaginary horn. Trust me, it doesn't take much to qualify as "exciting and noteworthy" when you're running on desolate roads all day.

The number one goal of each day was reaching the end of that day's run. I've always said this about long-distance runners: you have to wonder about doing something in which the best part is when you quit. The second goal was to eat a huge amount after the run was finished. Although I snacked all day, the feasting came in the evening when Mom, and later Marcy, prepared wonderful meals. The third goal was posting the day's summary on the website and getting and sending e-mail messages. Life was simple on the road, simple, at least, for me: run, eat, and exchange e-mails.

More soreness in the legs and the continued sore foot made for a slower, struggling day. I called it a day about one-half mile off I-40 in the middle of nowhere between Newberry Springs and Ludlow. After five days, the Bunion Derby runners had also stayed all night in the middle of nowhere, at a place called Mohave Wells. I never figured out where that place was located. For all I know, our motor home was parked exactly where Andy Payne's tent had been pitched.

After the first five days of the race, Payne had moved up to third place in the overall standings, his cumulative time over two hours behind the long-distance running legend Arthur Newton of South Africa. Although he was the next-to-youngest race entrant, Payne had surprised the sports writers with his pacing wisdom and race strategy. Of the 199 who started, only 155 remained in the race after five days.

Day 6, April 2.
Newberry Springs, CA to Bagdad, CA – 37.4 miles.
"Rashional Reaction"

ONLY THREE CARS passed by on the old Route 66 during the three hours it took to run 17 miles to Ludlow. Peaceful and alone, this was my type of run. Ludlow was the last town of any size for the next 100-plus miles, so we loaded up on food and supplies. I'm sure I looked strange to the locals as I stopped by the Ludlow Café in my running attire and gobbled up three huge pancakes.

Knowing we were leaving civilization for a few days, Dad went to the local gas station to fill up both in gasoline and water. The gasoline was no problem other than the price, but the service station attendant balked at the water, which is a valuable commodity in the desert. Dad told him about our venture and our need of enough water to last the next three days. Thankfully, the attendant had enough compassion to let Dad fill up the motor home water tank.

From Ludlow, Route 66 veers south, away from I-40, and becomes very isolated. I finished the day in Bagdad, or what used to be Bagdad, at the same location where the Bunion Derby had finished its sixth day. Bagdad Café had been a swinging place a number of years ago. An old movie by the name of *Bagdad Café* was made about it. Well, it's an old movie now; I guess it wasn't old when it was made. One scraggly old tree is the only thing that marks the spot where Bagdad once existed. Fire, drought, and time have reduced Bagdad to a small section of blacktop, a foundation of a building, and a few old relics that Dad and I explored that evening.

The medical mysteries of long-distance running continued as a red (aren't most of them) rash appeared on my feet and ankles by the end of the run. That, coupled with the first hint of a shin splint on the left leg and the normal swollen feet at the end of the day, reminded me to take it one day at a time and to trust that the Lord would give me strength and protection.

We were too far removed from civilization to make a phone connection, so I had to be content reflecting on earlier e-mails. I knew my home church, Sapulpa Bible Church, was supporting me. David Pritz had sent this e-mail a couple of days earlier: "We've got detailed maps up on the walls at church of every state you're running through along with weather reports and your updates — so this will really help to keep it all current and allow church members to follow the maps to see what the terrain is like and follow the internet weather reports to see what kind of weather you're facing — and, of course, to PRAY!"

This, as well as all the encouraging e-mails, was a good reminder of how powerful encouraging words can be. We do not realize how much of an influence we can be in people's lives when we take the time and initiative to be an encourager. One of

What's left of Bagdad, California, in the Mojave Desert: only a single tree.

life's most difficult challenges is to set aside our selfishness long enough to serve others. *"... whoever desires to become great among you shall become your servant, and whoever of you desires to be first shall be slave of all. For even the Son of Man did not come to be served, but to serve, and give His life a ransom for many"* (Mark 10:43-45).

Day 7, April 3.
Bagdad, CA to Essex, CA — 39.6 miles.
"Marriage on the Rocks"

EIGHT MILES INTO the day, I reached a wide spot in the road known as Amboy. Amboy consists of a gas station and a small school, which draws children from who knows how many miles. The population of Amboy is 12. The three people at the station meant that 25 percent of the town was there to greet me when I ran through, the highest percentage of any town I ran through.

After a phone call to Marcy at the pay phone, I left Amboy

behind — or so I thought. After 30 minutes of running, I turned around and it looked as though I was just a few blocks from Amboy. Another 30 minutes of running and Amboy was still very much visible behind me. The vastness and flatness of the desert became very evident as I felt as though Amboy was following me down the road. It took nearly three hours to "escape" the sight of Amboy.

Throughout the desert, people had written their names on hillsides using white rocks, which were in abundant supply. During one of my short breaks early in the day, I climbed a hill close to the road and spelled out my wife's name, "Marcy," with white rocks in about four-foot-tall letters. It somehow seemed strange to be gathering rocks and working on a hillside in the middle of a 40-mile running day. Mom took some pictures of me with my handiwork. I have often wondered if there's any semblance of my artwork left.

Though I had covered more miles this day than any previous day, it wasn't without a price. Normally, I took only a few short

Old Route 66 in the Mojave Desert.

walking breaks during each day; however, today I had walked all of the last four miles into the tiny community of Essex, my finish line for the day. Although the bottoms of my feet were better, the right quad muscle had become painful and made running difficult.

It now had been one week of running, and I had totaled 256.6 miles. The Bunion Derby runners had totaled 239.4 miles in one week. Though I had done some high-mileage training weeks, I had never put together a week like this. This was new ground for me. In planning the run, I had anticipated averaging about 32 miles per day. During this first week, I had averaged 36.5 miles per day and was nearly one day ahead of my expected pace. As I pondered the first week, together with its aches and pains, I wondered whether my body was breaking down. Had I pushed too hard?

Day 8, April 4.
Essex, CA to Rt. 66/H-95, CA — 34.2 miles.
"Getting a Leg Up"

LEAVING ESSEX, THE old Route 66 eventually veered back north, going over I-40 and through the tiny town of Goff. Some of this section of old Route 66 was no longer maintained and was very rough.

After walking the first two and one-half miles in the morning to loosen up, I ran well until about the 22-mile mark. The next 12 miles were a run/walk struggle, with the day ending prematurely on account of the painful right quad muscle. A premature ending allowed more time for the rice acronym on the right leg: rest (not really possible when running daily), ice, compression, and elevation.

In my diary notes that night, I wrote: "Kind of down — maybe because leg is bothering and limiting miles. Maybe just the reality of the endeavor." Though trying to stay upbeat around

An old portion of Route 66 near Goff, California, that is no longer maintained. Note the gloves: so, this is sunny California?

Dad and Mom, I was discouraged. However, the Lord would provide encouragement in two ways.

The previous three nights we had not been able to get a dial-up connection and receive e-mails. This night we drove into Needles to spend the night and were able to get a connection. We had 28 e-mail messages to read! The second encouragement was to come the next morning, Sunday.

Day 9, April 5.
Rt. 66/H-95, CA to near Oatman, AZ — 31.0 miles.
"Getting the Point"

OUTBACK RUNNING WAS the order of the day. Trying to navigate the 13 miles to Needles, the last town in California, turned into a true cross-country adventure. Trying to avoid a six-mile stretch of running on I-40, I ran on a dirt road somewhat adjacent to the busy interstate highway. Although the dirt road began veering away, I was assured by a hippie couple, stranded beside a broken-down car, that the dirt road would lead to Needles.

After more veering away from I-40, I began to wonder just

how much you could trust the directions of a hippie couple who themselves looked lost. Fearing I could end up in Nevada at the rate I was leaving I-40, I decided to leave the dirt road and set off across the desert-like country towards Needles, which could vaguely be seen in the distance. I quickly learned that the best way to dodge cacti, sagebrush and boulders was by trying to walk through washed-out gullies where possible. I would climb out of the gullies occasionally to get the right alignment toward Needles and then go back down into the gully and navigate a little further.

However, I wasn't totally successful at avoiding the cacti. On one of my out-of-the-gully experiences, a long cactus needle stuck through the top canvas part of my running shoe, bloodying a toe. It was then that the name "Needles" made perfect sense for this town, if you get my point. After about thirty minutes of cross-country cactus whacking and a little worse for the wear, it was nice to get back to pavement.

In Needles, we found a local church to attend. Interim pastor Tommy Thompson of First Baptist Church of Needles introduced me and asked me to share a few words about my trip. The congregation was friendly and encouraging, just what I needed following yesterday's discouragement.

After church, it was out of the dress clothes and back into the running attire. Leaving Needles, I crossed the Colorado River Bridge and entered Arizona. As what became customary when entering a new state, we stopped for pictures. I took off my sunglasses to pose for the pictures on the bridge. Apparently giddy over completing the California crossing, it was three miles down the road before I realized that my sunglasses were still on the bridge. I'm sure the sunglasses were disappointed to come 322 miles across California and not be able to continue the journey. They would have been even more disappointed had they known they were replaced by a cheap pair from an Arizona convenience store three miles down the road.

Randy and his father, Calvin, sharing a few (s)miles together.

Randy on Route 66 in the desolate Mojave Desert.

4

DOES ANYONE REALLY KNOW WHAT TIME IT IS?

Day 10, April 6.
Near Oatman, AZ to Kingman, AZ — 38.0 miles.
"Road Crossings"

VACATING CALIFORNIA AND entering Arizona, old Route 66 goes through Sitgreaves Pass, an elevation of 3,550 feet, on its way to the town of Oatman. The views were beautiful, which made the long uphill climb easier to handle. Oatman was an old mining town that had been made into a small tourist town. Burros still roam the street, walk on the wooden sidewalks, and stick their heads into doorways, where shop owners run them out of the shop.

Oatman looks like something you would see in the old western movies – and you may have. "How the West Was Won," "Grapes of Wrath," and several other movies were filmed in part there, or so we were told.

The first few miles of the day were a constant uphill climb as I mixed running and walking. This part was scenic and enjoyable. However, the descent was a different story. The right quad, which had been bothersome a few days earlier, began to ache from the downhill pounding. So far, I had not been taking any pain medication. The holdout ended as I took two ibuprofren several different times on the downhills in order to ease the pain until I was able to get to flatter country near Kingman.

The roadside crosses always caught my attention as I ran across the country. The previous day I saw a cross for Tammy who died at seven years of age and Brock who died at 18, which made me think of my 19-year-old daughter, Heather. I never passed a cross without wondering about the circumstances of the death and the grieving families left behind. The two crosses to-day, which particularly caught my attention, were "Fat Boy Harley Rider — 39" and "Road Hard." They apparently didn't make one of the sharp curves that are common near Sitgreaves Pass.

Arriving at Kingman, Arizona, I was excited to realize that I had run 360 miles in 10 days. The Bunion Derby had also made it to Kingman in 10 days in 346 miles. My route out of Los Angeles and through the Needles area was a few miles longer than the Bunion Derby race.

As we settled into a KOA campground, I wondered where the Bunion Derby runners and entourage had slept on this night in Kingman. One thing is known: Payne had moved up to sec-ond place over all, but trailed Newton by nearly seven hours in cumulative time. The miles, heat, and hills had taken a toll on the field; after 10 days, only 110 of the 199 starters remained in the race.

Day 11, April 7.
Kingman, AZ to Truxton, AZ — 39.0 miles.
"Keep On Truxton"

EXITING KINGMAN ON Route 66, the first 18 miles were as straight as a string before reaching the foothills. Route 66 stole my heart as I ran through the small old towns of Hackberry and

Valentine. I finished in Truxton, which has an elevation of 4,300 feet, a gain of 1,000 feet from the start of the day in Kingman. The temperature dropped after about 30 miles and it started to sprinkle. I donned my Gore-Tex™ running suit, and soon the rain turned to snow. I felt like a kid skipping down the road as snow flurries splattered my black jacket. During the last five miles into Truxton, there was a rain/snow storm in the large valley below me to the right. The various shades of blue, gray, and white formed a beautiful curtain stretching from the clouds to the valley floor. God's beautiful handiwork was on display for much of the run today.

At day's end, we ate dinner at the Frontier Motel/Café, a long-time fixture on Route 66. I'm not sure which is the oldest fixture, the café or the 92-year-old man from Tahlequah, Oklahoma, who appeared to be the owner. After many miles of solitude and little conversation, listening to him during the entire meal made up for lost time.

I often have been asked what I ate on the run. The answer is most anything we could get and lots of it. This night I ate a hamburger, French fries, grilled-cheese sandwich, potato chips and a chocolate shake. And as usual, less than two hours later I was eating again in the motor home. To all of you who are shaking your head over the quality of that meal: yes, I usually ate healthier than this.

Mom wrote in her journal: "He eats bagels and granola bars during pit stops and a little cereal before he starts, but at the end of the day, he makes up for it. It's fun to cook for him because he is so hungry after running all day that he really enjoys it." Mom couldn't have had as much fun cooking as I did eating. The wonderful meals were a major reason for being able to put in as many miles as I did.

I continued to avoid the heat that I had dreaded. After a cool day, the low temperature hit 32 degrees on this night.

Day 12, April 8.
Truxton, AZ to Seligman, AZ — 39.8 miles.
"Time Off"

DETERMINED TO EAT breakfast at the Frontier Café, we were waiting at the front door at 6 a.m., the time they said they would be open. We waited around a few minutes for the place to open, but no one came to open up. Finally, at 6:15 I took off on the day's run. They had been such nice folks the previous night; we were puzzled as to why they had assured us they would be open at 6 a.m. and then didn't show up.

The answer to the puzzle became embarrassingly evident the next morning. When we had entered Arizona four days earlier, we had advanced our watches two hours: one hour for Pacific to the Mountain time zone and one hour for daylight savings time which had taken effect that day. At Lilo's Restaurant in Seligman, five days after entering Arizona, we inquired as to why their clock "was wrong," only to find out Arizona does not change its time when the rest of the nation goes onto daylight savings time. We had been an hour off the correct Arizona time for four days and had not realized it. Therefore, we had been standing in front of the Frontier Café at 5 a.m. the previous morning, not 6 a.m. as we had thought. The song, "Does Anyone Really Know What Time It Is," went through my mind several times.

There were beautiful views this day as Route 66 climbed from 4,300 feet to an elevation of 5,500 feet. For the first time, I noticed a bit of thinness to the air as breathing became a little labored at times. Breathing also became difficult for two very cute puppies who tried to join me today. Though they tried to stay with me, it was not very long before their short legs could no longer keep pace.

One highlight of the day was climbing over a fence into cow-pasture land and running one and a half miles on some of the original Route 66 pavement poured in the 1920s. This old sec-

In front of the "home away from home" — Randy with his wonderful crew: parents Calvin and Hazel Ellis.

tion had a thin layer of crumbling old-time reddish asphalt laid over a gravel bed. Weeds and shrubs had grown up in the road — not to mention the numerous cow patties that constantly had to be sidestepped.

For the past three weeks, I had been in my own world and had no clue as to how the stock market or my former employer's stock was doing. Included in the e-mails this day was one from the unknown Greek Affairs staff at LSU stating, "Good Luck and Godspeed on your fantastic endeavor. I hope you perform better than Parker Drilling's stock has the last few weeks (just kidding)."

Day 13, April 9.
Seligman, AZ to near Williams, AZ — 43.4 miles.
"Keeping Track"

I'M NOT SURE if it was finding out the right time or if it was the strain of the first 11 miles, but the three large pancakes consumed for breakfast at Lilo's did not sit well. I'm not known for having a particularly strong stomach, but there had been no trouble to this point. However, the first three hours of this day was a nauseous mixture of walking and trying to run. I now knew for sure that not eating large breakfasts before running had been the best strategy.

In addition to an upset stomach, I also was disappointed in not getting to meet Mr. Route 66, Angel Delgadillo, owner of Delgadillo memorabilia and barbershop in downtown Seligman. I had been told that I needed to stop in and meet the man who knew a great deal about the history of Route 66. However, due to my early-morning start, I ran through Seligman hours before he would open his shop. Nearly four years later, Dad and Mom would stop by his shop on a trip to California and tell him about my run and disappointment in not getting to meet him. He sent with them an autographed drawing of his barbershop to give to me.

Today was the day that I had dreaded from the start: Route 66 doesn't exist for the 47 miles from Ash Fork to Flagstaff. The only apparent alternative was to run on Interstate 40 with its heavy traffic.

For safety purposes, a runner runs against the traffic on the left side of the road. The shoulder of the highway is generally about six feet wide. That doesn't leave much room between a pedestrian and the speeding missiles. Trucks and cars whizzing by within six feet at 75 to 80 miles per hour can be unnerving. The passing of large trucks create a blast of air that would nearly halt me in mid-stride. Stride, stride, blast, pause, stand up straight, lean forward, stride, stride, blast. It was a pattern that was to be repeated thousands of times.

To stay off I-40, I would run on almost any other road or surface that was available. On this day, I pushed the envelope too far. Leaving Ash Fork, there was a railroad track with a dirt road beside it running alongside I-40. A local resident had told me that the railroad track goes from Ash Fork to Williams, my intended destination for the day. In order to stay off I-40, I made the decision to stay on the dirt road next to the tracks and follow the tracks to Williams.

After a few minutes of running, the train track and its adjacent dirt road began to veer north away from I-40. I wasn't concerned because I could still see I-40. After a few more minutes of running, I couldn't see I-40, but I could still hear the traffic. I was now a little concerned. A few more minutes of running and I could just barely hear the traffic. I was now a little more concerned. It wasn't long before I could hear nothing, and now the tracks and the dirt road and I were in the middle of wilderness. My concern had grown to the moderate range.

Now what? I chose to continue running, hoping the tracks would veer back south toward I-40. After about another 30 minutes of running alongside the tracks, and not even a faint sound of traffic, I was very concerned. I thought, "I have no idea where I am. At this rate, am I going to end up in Utah?" Since I had been running for at least an hour since I had left Ash Fork, it was difficult to think about retracing my steps and losing the progress I hoped I had made. However, if I continued along the tracks, who knows how much progress I might eventually lose? Retracing my steps now may be better than less-attractive alternatives such as never finding civilization again and being eaten by wild animals.

While pondering my plight and praying about what to do, I ran around a bend and saw a railroad employee who had driven out to work on the tracks. Was he ever surprised to see a runner out in the middle of the wilderness! Was I ever surprised to see a railroad worker in the middle of the wilderness! I was so happy to see someone, anyone, that to him I must have seemed like a lost dog that finds his owner.

He directed me to a rutted-out old trail that went across pastures and streams and eventually led back to I-40. It was a three-hour adventure from Ash Fork until I finally reached I-40. As much as I disdained I-40, it never looked better than it did when I finally saw it across the pastureland. As I climbed the embankment to reach the highway, I now willingly resigned myself to running on I-40. It had won the battle this day.

I was soon found by a very worried Dad and Mom, who had been driving up and down I-40 not having a clue as to where I could be. We called it a day at mileage marker 154 and drove several miles into Williams to spend the night. Per Mom's journal, "Tonight was the most tired I have seen Randy since he started." No argument from me.

After I wrote about the day's adventure on the website, friend Mike Jeffries later e-mailed, "Leave it to you to take a long cut on a 3000-mile run." I'm quite sure the Bunion Derby runners did not have the off-highway adventures on their 13th day when they finished in Williams. The Bunion Derby runners and I were nearly even in miles: I had run 482 miles as compared to the 480 miles for the Bunion Derby runners. In the overall race standings, Arthur Newton had stretched his lead over second place Andy Payne to over eight hours. Was the pre-race favorite going to win in a rout on a route — Route 66?

Day 14, April 10.
Williams, AZ to Flagstaff, AZ — 40.0 miles.
"Needing a Leg To Stand On"

THE PREVIOUS DAY'S "off-track" run into the wilderness had added an extra six miles, I estimated. At the end of the day yesterday, Dad suggested that we could add the six miles to where I had stopped and I could start on up the highway at mileage marker 160 instead of 154.

Being frustrated at myself and disappointed at having run an estimated six miles that didn't gain any distance across the country, I went to sleep contemplating Dad's suggestion. However, I woke up in the middle of the night and realized that I would always be disappointed if I did not resume exactly where I left off the previous day. How could I say I ran across the country if I skipped six miles on I-40? I realized then more than ever that doing the right thing is often not easy, but never regretted. With renewed determination in the morning, we drove back to mileage post 154 and resumed the journey. Though it was mostly on I-40 all day, it was a gorgeous run with pine trees, patches of snow and two beautiful snow-covered peaks north of Flagstaff. It was gorgeous, but difficult, as I climbed against a headwind to the Arizona Divide at 7,337 feet and finished in Flagstaff where we camped in snow-covered Woody Campground RV Park. The Bunion Derby runners also stayed overnight in Flagstaff on their 14th day. However, they did not stay in Woody Campground (as though it existed then). Race accounts state that it was one of the few nights they had inside accommodations. On most nights they erected large tents and the runners slept on cots.

I felt blessed to reach the 500-mile mark during the run today. It was encouraging when I ran by a big sign on I-40 during the day to turn around and see "Los Angeles 474." It made me realize that the daily effort was indeed resulting in tangible progress.

I was made even more thankful when I met Lester Burnett at a rest stop on I-40 during the run. Lester was hitchhiking from Kentucky to California to get a new leg prosthesis to replace his worn-out one. After we talked for a few minutes, he shook my hand, took my picture and wished me well. Realizing the seriousness of his hike put my "joy run" in a different perspective. I knew that anything I faced on my journey would be light and momentary compared to his cross-country journey in order to get a new leg. *"For our light affliction, which is but for a moment, is working for us a far more exceedingly and eternal weight of glory"* (II Corinthians 4:17).

Day 15, April 11.
Flagstaff, AZ to Two Guns, AZ — 32.5 miles.
"Winded"

HERE HE COMES, running along with the tumbling tumbleweeds — and tumbling pinecones and tumbling caterpillars. I only thought that yesterday was a tough running day. During this day, I ran in the strongest winds in which I have ever run. Pine cones were literally bouncing across the road in Flagstaff. Caterpillar-like creatures were being wind blown out of the pine trees and across the road. It's no exaggeration when I say that I saw a tumbleweed about the size of a Volkswagen blow across the road and bang into a fence. Cans, trash — there was no telling what might come blowing across the road.

For much of the day I was running on I-40. Several times, the 40-50-miles-per-hour wind gusts from the south would actually blow me off the side of the road and part way down the embankment alongside the road. Often, I would be blown two steps to the left, then tilt, lean and weave my way back to the right. The wind, plus the additional blasts from the large trucks, made for one of the most difficult days of the run. By the time I reached 32 miles, I was one wind-whipped, staggering puppy, ready to call it a day.

Early in the day I had put layers of vaseline and sunblock on my legs to protect from the little flying missiles of gravel and dirt that would sting my legs. Unfortunately, the vaseline and sunblock made a great adhesive. By day's end, my legs were covered with a thick layer of dirt and grit. The shower stall at the RV Park in Two Guns was probably never the same after I scrubbed and scrubbed and scrubbed.

The wind did not diminish in the evening and rocked the motor home all night. I prayed that the winds would diminish before morning. I wasn't sure how much more of this "fun" I could stand. As it turned out, tomorrow was much better, but the damage had been done.

Day 16, April 12.
Two Guns, AZ to Winslow, AZ — 32.0 miles.
"Cop Out"

Easter MORNING! THE morning was cool with a light rain, but the wind was not nearly as strong. Much better running conditions!

Early in the morning as I ran on I-40, an Arizona highway patrolman pulled over and stopped in front of me. There are signs on many I-40 entrance ramps that clearly say, "No pedestrians allowed." Dad and Mom found the police station in Williams three days earlier, and there they called the highway patrol office to explain my run and ask permission to run on I-40. Though the patrolman on the phone said okay to their request, I now dreaded talking to this patrolman on the side of the road.

As I ran up to the passenger window, I wondered what he thought of a grown man running in the middle of nowhere in the rain early on Easter morning. I thought he might get out the breath analyzer to check for a DUI, or would that be a RUI — running under the influence.

He asked "Out for a jog?"

I said, "Yes, sir, you might say that. But you aren't going to believe this when I tell you." I proceeded to explain my run and that we had called the highway patrol office when we were in Williams.

He just shook his head and said, "Well, at least you're on the correct side of the road. Be careful." He had seen many things, I'm sure; but I suspect that our encounter was a first for him. I could imagine him telling his wife that night, "Honey, you're not going to believe this one; now I've heard it all."

After running about 20 miles in the morning, we drove into Winslow and located a church for an Easter worship service. Later in the day when I reached Winslow on my run, we stopped and stood on the corner in Winslow for some pictures. Seriously, there is a store named "Standing on the Corner in Winslow, Arizona."

During the last few miles through Winslow, I was developing a sore right shin. I later realized that this was the damage done in the wind the previous day. During the previous day, my stride had been continually affected by the strong wind. Additionally, there were those times where I had been blown part way down the embankment off the side of the road. Due to the camber (I just had to use that tricky word, which means slope) of the road, the right leg was the uphill leg. I'm not necessarily sure why, but the right leg must have taken the brunt of the toll. The pain in the shin at the end of this, my 16th day, was an omen that the biggest challenge of the run lay just ahead.

Incredibly, the way Andy Payne's 16th day ended was also an omen that the biggest challenge of his run lay just ahead. On the 16th day, the Bunion Derby runners ran one of their shortest segments, 24.1 miles from Two Gun Camp to Winslow. Even though it was a short distance, Payne had run at a pace slower than normal, struggling to a 17th place finish for this day's segment. The reason for his slow time would become apparent the next day.

Although his run had been disappointingly slow, Andy Payne did receive the biggest break of his Bunion Derby race on this 16th day. The Bunion Derby reporters were abuzz when they received the news that Arthur Newton, the leader by over nine hours, dropped out of the race six miles before Winslow. The 44-year-old Newton simply said that his legs were dead. Maybe he had pushed too hard in recent months. One month earlier, he had set the world record for the 100-mile run, covering the distance in 14 hours, 22 minutes.

As surprised as everyone was over Newton's departure, they were just as surprised that Andy Payne was now the race leader, having over a one-hour margin over Arne Souminen. Before the race began, no one had given the 19-year-old Cherokee Indian a chance to win. When Andy was asked if he had a new strategy now that he was leading, he replied, "Just going to keep stepping along for the time being."

5

TAKING IT ON THE SHIN

Day 17, April 13.
Winslow, AZ to Holbrook, AZ — 33.0 miles.
"Taking It on the Shin"

I WAS OFF to my earliest start of the journey, stepping out of the motor home at 5:30 in the morning. From the first step down the steps, my right shin ached every time I landed on my right foot. Any downhill grade was almost intolerable. The shin was red and the swelling extended down into the ankle.

Every time I stopped to rest, it was very difficult to get started again. After hobbling a little ways, the shin would loosen up somewhat and I could run a little. I would put on my best game face around Dad and Mom, knowing they were concerned. However, as soon as I was out of their sight, I would have to fight back the tears from the pain. I kept thinking that if it didn't get any worse, I could keep going. On the other hand, I knew shin splints don't get better if you walk/run 33 miles per day on them.

I tried to remain positive by thinking, "At least it's only one leg; every other step feels good." That was the line I put on my website that night as I asked for prayers. I tried to put on the game face by never telling anyone how difficult and painful this day was. I knew more than ever that it was only by God's strength that I made the 33 miles to Holbrook. Dad wrote in his journal, "I had to congratulate him on his determination but it may have been too much on a bad leg."

In an attempt to ignore the pain, I spent much of the day thinking about the Bunion Derby runners, who were doing the same Winslow to Holbrook segment on the exact same 17th day. More specifically, on my toughest running day I thought often about Andy Payne. For the first 16 days, I felt as though I had "run with Payne" by running some of the same segments and nearly the same amount of total miles.

As much as Andy Payne's and my runs had paralleled each other for the first 16 days, it was now almost unbelievable how much our 17th days were alike. I continue to marvel at the similarity. Not only had we both started in Winslow and ended in Holbrook, but we also shared a common bond in that the 17th day had been Andy Payne's toughest running day also.

Andy showed up at the start line on the morning of March 20,1928 in Winslow, Arizona with tonsillitis. His slow time the previous day had been an indication that he was not feeling well. Payne had been a model of consistency until then, but now, being ill, he was at a distinct disadvantage.

Race officials told the reporters that they did not think Andy would finish this day's 34.3-miles segment to Holbrook. However, he doggedly ran and walked to Holbrook, finishing three hours behind the leaders. He now had relinquished the lead, but he was still in the race. I feel positive that Payne laid in bed that night, relieved to have finished the day, but very worried about the upcoming days. I knew I did. It had been a day of running with pain, as well as with Payne.

Day 18, April 14.
Day off.
"Off and On"

WORST DAY — THIS was the longest and worst day of the run, and I didn't run a step. After discussing it with Dad and Mom, I reluctantly agreed to take a day off and see if the shin splint would improve. However, being a veteran runner, I knew that one day off would not heal a serious injury.

We did some sight-seeing, including a museum and the famous Route 66 Wigwam Motel. Basically, we just killed time and tried not to think about the fact that we were not making any easterly headway. Dad went to a parts store and bought a compass to go in the motor home. Given my penchant for off-road excursions, I told Dad that I needed the compass fixed to my hat, not to the motor home. We had to look for levity wherever we could find it. It was a depressing day.

A friend, David Pritz, had called KRMG, the largest radio station in Tulsa, Oklahoma, and told them about my run. John Erling, the morning radio personality, sent word through David to have me call them and give them live updates. I had called the previous morning, but due to the time difference it had not worked and they were not able to interview me on the radio.

This morning, I found a phone booth at the RV park and was interviewed live on the air with John Erling. This was to become a Monday morning ritual for the remainder of the run. It was with mixed feelings I talked on radio that morning, excited to have covered 620 miles, but disappointed to tell them I was taking a day off due to a shin splint. I was sure that many listeners figured that my journey was about to end; by God's help, I was determined to prove them wrong.

It was a depressing day, but God always provides encouragement when times are dark. The previous day, I had written on my website about the shin splint and had asked for advice on treatment. I received this e-mail from Captain Joe McClung: "I am a Captain in the U.S. Army serving as an Armor Officer in 4-64 Armor here in the 3rd Infantry Division at Fort Stewart, Georgia ... You can rest assured that I will specifically add you, by name, into my daily prayers. You are an inspiration, and I will use your mission as a teaching tool to my soldiers to show them what you can do with a goal and desire to excel. I wish you God's speed for success and safety in your journey." Captain McClung went on to give some very helpful suggestions for treating a shin splint. Wow! After reading that e-mail, how could a person not be ready to resume the battle first thing the next morning?

Though I had taken the day off, Andy did not have that luxury. Fighting the effects of tonsillitis, he showed up at the start line on this 18th day and struggled to complete the 40-mile segment. However, he finished well behind the leaders. Not only had he relinquished the lead, but he was now losing time and positions in the overall standings.

It had been a thrill to run from Santa Monica to Holbrook, Arizona in the same 17 days that the Bunion Derby covered that same distance. Now it was disheartening to know that the Bunion Derby had gotten off to an early start this morning and had left me behind. I was left thinking that I would never again be on the same pace with them.

Day 19, April 15.
Holbrook, AZ to Navajo, AZ – 37.0 miles.
"Forgive Us Our Trespasses"

OUR INTENTIONS WERE to get up at 5:30 a.m. and get an early start in order to resume running this morning. It was still really dark when Dad woke us up. I squinted at my watch and saw that it was 4:30 a.m. Dad must have been more eager than I to get me back to running: he had misread his watch and awakened us an hour early.

It felt nice to resume the journey after a day off. It felt nice in one sense, but not so nice in another sense. Based on some advice I received from e-mails, we tried taping the shin; however, the shin began to ache shortly after starting. After hobbling a ways, it would warm up and loosen enough to shuffle down the road. The shin was swollen down into the ankle, making it painful to flex the foot. I minimized the flexing and pain as much as possible by stiffly shuffling, which was less painful than walking, though not much faster.

Knowing I liked the movie "What About Bob?" my brother Craig borrowed a few lines when he e-mailed, "Keep doing the work and don't be a slacker and baby-step your way to the Atlantic." My slow shuffle sure seemed like baby steps; it seemed to take forever to make any easterly headway this day.

It was a cold, windy day with the wind coming mostly behind me from the southwest. It was actually too strong at times and would blow me at a faster pace than my desired pain-minimizing shuffle pace.

Getting across Arizona was difficult due to the number of miles that I had to run on I-40. To avoid the highway as much as possible, I would run on adjacent dirt roads, trails, cow trails, fields, nearly anything that was passable. I had climbed so many fences that I had actually gotten a sore right palm from placing it on top of the metal fence posts when climbing over. Friend Ed Swift of Sapulpa e-mailed, "From your description of some of your running, are you training for a steeplechase?"

On this day, I had gotten off I-40, climbed a fence and was running across vacant land. Eventually my path went in front of a house and down a driveway that led away from the house. Running in front of the house, I had to make a decision as to whether to climb back over the fence onto I-40 or continue running across someone's private property. It didn't look as though anyone was home, so I decided to take my chances running across private property. Wrong choice!

As I was running out through a gate, leaving the private property and heading for public property, the owners of the house came driving up the road. They were rather rude and forceful as they asked me what I was doing on their land. I was almost relieved to be threatened with calling the authorities and being arrested. I considered that a better alternative than those country folks taking the law in their own hands.

Proverbs 15:1 says, *"A soft answer turns away wrath."* I told them I was running across the country and had made a mistake by getting off I-40. I apologized for being on their property. Their anger subsided and they even offered some directions on how to get to my destination town of Navajo without having to get back on the highway. I didn't climb as many fences after this, nor attempt as many "off-road" excursions.

After a few snow flurries during the day, the snow came blowing in during the evening. The empty lot where we parked quickly turned into a white winter wonderland. Where's the heat? We had been on the road for 19 days and because of the cool, sometimes cold, temperatures, we had used our lawn chairs only twice, and then just briefly in the afternoon after finishing the day's run.

Though concerned about what lay ahead, I felt gratified knowing that I had given my best effort this day by hobbling through 37 miles. I was sure that 70 years ago there was a young Cherokee Indian who had struggled through 34.7 miles, battling tonsillitis on his 19th day, and had probably felt the same way.

Day 20, April 16.
Navajo, AZ to Lupton, AZ — 34.5 miles.
"Twilight Zona"

RUNNING 37 MILES the previous day on a swollen shin and ankle caused me to be very apprehensive about this day. It was again cold; however, it wasn't as windy. The pain of running was about the same as the previous day. I considered it a good sign that 37 miles the previous day had not made it any worse. However, Mom's journal entry for the day concluded with the statement, "I'm really worried about Randy's leg." Mom would never know that we were in complete harmony on that topic. Oh, I guess she will now.

Although the shin splint had not gotten better, I was encouraged nevertheless. I had received numerous e-mails saying that they were praying for me. Several e-mails were from coaches or people who knew how to treat shin splints. I received much advice and several articles on how to ice and tape shin splints. Dad and I probably tried about everything we received. It was tremendously uplifting to feel as though many family, friends, and strangers from all over the country had come to my rescue. And, of course, I believed that it was all orchestrated by the great Rescuer, Jesus Christ Himself.

This day's journey went through the small towns of Chambers and Sanders, ending at 6,000-feet elevation in Lupton on the Arizona/New Mexico state line. After several days of desert scenery, the red rock cliffs and canyons were a welcome change. It had been a struggle, but it was a moral victory to have another state behind me.

What was even better was having the longest stretch of running on I-40 now behind me. There had been very little remaining of Route 66 from Ash Fork (45 miles west of Flagstaff) to 12 miles from the New Mexico state line. Of that 160-mile stretch, I estimated that I had avoided, not always successfully, about half of it by my fence climbings and "off-road endeavors."

Undoubtedly, Andy Payne did not have as many off-road adventures as I did; however, he did have a good 20th day. He was on his way to recovery from tonsillitis and finished 7th in this day's 32.8-mile segment.

Day 21, April 17.
Lupton, AZ to Gallup, NM — 31.1 miles.
"What the Doctor Ordered"

LIMPING AROUND THE motor home, I found it difficult to get started this morning. It took about eight miles to get loosened up and be able to run somewhat better. After rest breaks, it was always difficult to get the shin and ankle loosened up; therefore, I kept the rest breaks short and far between. I figured I might as well keep hobbling at my slow pace if I was going to cover very many miles.

In the morning, Dad and Mom came up with a good plan. They drove on ahead into Gallup, New Mexico and called longtime family friend Lila Smith in Tulsa, assistant to their family doctor, Dr. Paul Hendrix. Dad and Mom explained the situation and symptoms, and Dr. Hendrix phoned a prescription for some strong anti-inflammatory medicine to a Walgreen's drug store in Gallup. Though always reluctant to take much medicine, I did not have to be coerced to begin taking the medication that afternoon. I was hoping and praying for some relief. Though running with Payne had been a thrill, running with pain had diminished the joy of the journey the past four days.

The red rock cliffs and bluffs were gorgeous during this part of the run. They were also deceiving. Several times a train would be coming along the south side to my right. The sound would echo off the tall bluffs to my left and sound for certain like the train was north of me. I learned that you can't always trust everything you hear.

We spent the night in Red Rock State Park just east of Gallup, one of the nicest and prettiest places in which we stayed during the run. Dad spent part of the evening climbing and exploring the surrounding hills. After one night of not being able to get a phone connection, we were able to dial in and connect to the website. Waiting were 22 messages that provided a great amount of much-appreciated encouragement.

At this point in my run, I had covered 722 miles, about 18 miles less than the Bunion Derby. They were spending this night in Thoreau, a small town through which I would run the next day. My shin splint seemed to be getting a little better; but Andy's tonsillitis was much better. He had finished third on Day 21's segment and was now back in second place, but over three hours behind Souminen.

Day 22, April 18.
Gallup, NM to Prewitt, NM — 33.5 miles.
"Crash Training"

DETERMINED TO PRESS on, I made it over the top today: up and over the Continental Divide, elevation of 7,300 feet. I surely wasn't complaining, but I thought the Rocky Mountain Divide was at least 8,000 feet in elevation. As it turned out, its actual elevation was nearly the same as the Arizona Divide near Flagstaff.

One of the memorable things about a cross-country journey is the interesting people that one meets. Today at Exit 44 on I-40, I met truck drivers Jimmy Dye and his wife, taking a break and walking their dog. He was really interested in my story and told me about his former days as a marathon runner.

The early miles seemed a little easier today; hopefully the medicine was working. I ran through the Route 66 towns of Thoreau and Prewitt and ended the day at the site of an apparent train crash a few years earlier just outside of Prewitt. There were several mangled train cars still strewn about. It was appropriate to end the day's run here: the train and I had crashed at the same exact spot. The wear and tear of the past few days had taken a toll.

As tired as I was at the end of the day, the good news was that my shin and foot looked somewhat less red and swollen than it had at the end of the previous four running days. Though worn out, the diminished pain during the day encouraged me. I was amazed that I had run 137 miles in four days and a red, swollen shin and ankle had actually gotten better! I can certainly understand someone being skeptical when they read this — I'm sure I would be, too, if I had not experienced it. I was amazed then and I still am nearly seven years later. I know of only one answer: He Who made the shin.

On a sad note, Mom called home and found out that one of her best friends, and my third grade teacher, Francis Echols, had died the previous day. Before we had left home to drive to California, Mom had asked friends and family to commit to pray often for me on certain dates. Mrs. Echols had signed the calendar on June 19 as the day she would specifically pray for me. However, the Lord had determined that her homecoming would take place before that date. Being on the road tended to isolate us from real life; but occasionally something like Mrs. Echols' death would remind us that we were temporarily living in a dream, and not in the reality of life.

I had completed 755 miles and the weather had been cool, if not downright cold most of the time. My diary noted that I had run in gloves all day today. Of course, that was not all; the diary failed to note that I also ran in a long-legged and long-sleeved running suit all day.

Day 23, April 19.
Prewitt, NM to Villa de Cubero, NM — 38.5 miles.
"Without Reservation"

THIS TURNED OUT to be a glorious day on two accounts. First, it was sunny, cloudless, and windless with a high near 70 degrees. This was the first day in over a week that I ran in shorts and a short-sleeve shirt. As Mom wrote in her diary at the end of the day, "It's been a great day!"

However, most important and most amazing, I ran with much less pain all day. It went so well, I was able to cover 38.5 miles even though we took a two-hour break to attend church on this Sunday morning. This was the morning that the greeter at the church accused me of being in the sun too long, which didn't bother me. Really, it didn't.

Nothing could dampen the excitement of being able to run again with only minimal pain. After six days of pain, and the nagging question of "will I be able to continue?", running with less pain was real cause for joy and thanksgiving. I have often told the story of how an inflamed and swollen shin and ankle could improve dramatically, and eventually get well, while it is being pounded upon for 30 to 40 miles a day. God truly honored the prayers of many people in a miraculous way — I would never have believed it unless I had experienced it.

Running with less physical pain, I felt as though I was again *Running With Payne*. I had actually regained ground on the Bunion Derby pace in the last five days and had now run 794 miles in 23 days, compared to its 805 miles in 23 days. On the 23rd night, the Bunion Derby runners were spending the night in Laguna, just eight miles up the road from where we are staying in Villa de Cubero. Payne was still in second place in the overall standings and still three hours behind Souminen.

We enjoyed meeting several Native American Indians during this stretch of the run. One man stopped to check on Dad and Mom as they waited for me; he wanted to make sure they weren't having motor home problems. They explained to him what we were doing. As he drove back up the road to where I was running, he slowed and hollered, "God be with you. I just wanted to tell you, God be with you."

When I reached our stopping place for the day, Dad and Mom were talking to Raymond Critchell, a Native American who had hitchhiked in from a nearby reservation. After meeting Dad and Mom, he had hung around the motor home for 30 minutes waiting for me to arrive. He introduced himself, shook my hand twice, offered encouragement and said, "God will be with you," as he left.

I was touched by the kindness of these people who had very little possessions or material things. That night I wrote this on my website, "I've noticed an indicting paradox. Those who have less possessions and goods often are more courteous, encouraging, and giving to complete strangers. Dear friends, may that never be said to be true about us who have been blessed so much!" Though certainly not always true, it was a pattern that was to repeat itself over and over again: those who have less are often the most willing to share what they do have.

Day 24, April 20.
Villa de Cubero, NM to Highway 6, NM — 37.9 miles.
"The Bunny Hop"

THE EXCITEMENT OF running better and farther yesterday must have caught up with me during the night, as I did not sleep well. That made for a long and tiring day as I ran through the small, definitely New Mexican, towns of Cubero, Casa Blanca, Laguna, New Laguna, and Laguna Pueblo.

After crossing over I-40 at mileage marker 119, I ran eight miles on an old, seldom-used portion of Route 66. Every few hundred yards, there were large red-ant hills on the road. Only two cars passed by during that eight miles of running. I was running in solitude when five feet in front of me, up jumped the largest jackrabbit I've ever seen. It looked like a mid-size dog with 10-inch ears sticking straight up. I'm not sure who was more startled, the rabbit or me.

I reached Highway 6, which skirts to the south of Albuquerque, and ran 12 miles on it toward Belen before calling it a day. Where we finished and parked for the night was very desolate. Dad explored the littered terrain that afternoon and gathered an assortment of rocks, tools, car parts, and other junk — treasures, that is.

It always made Mom nervous to spend the night away from civilization. I'm not sure she ever slept much on those nights, as she stayed awake to make sure strangers did not visit us. Dad and I did not seem to worry about the danger and would appreciate the quiet solitude. However, just thinking about it now makes me more nervous than I was then.

On the website this night was the following offer: "Randy, when you finish with the usa, you can come on down to oztralia and run across it (the scenery is great). keep it up — i'll be watching you progress, a mate from down under, john greydanus."

Even Mom had gotten into the Andy Payne spirit this day. I later read where she wrote in her diary, "Saw some old buildings and ruins — probably Andy Payne ran by them in 1928." All right, Mom. You've caught the fever!

After 24 days, the blisters or problems with the feet and toes became very minimal. However, this day I did have a sore toe. When I cut back the toenail that night with the clippers, fluid that had built up under the toe squirted about a foot into the air. I know, I know; you really didn't need that piece of information.

Day 25, April 21.
Highway 6, NM to Highway 47, NM — 38.5 miles.
"No Fee for All"

HAVING ENDURED ALL the cold and wind of the previous days made this one a particularly beautiful morning. The cool, dry air was so fresh and often included the scent of pine trees. The sunny, cloudless blue sky generally had two or three airplane vapor streaks across it.

The first 14 miles of the day was a gradual climb on Highway 6 before dropping into Los Lunas and the Rio Grande River valley south of Albuquerque. I had made the decision to depart from the Bunion Derby route for about the next 100 miles.

The Bunion Derby had gone north from Los Lunas, skirting east around Albuquerque before continuing on Route 66. The Bunion Derby race director had refused to run the race through Albuquerque after the town refused to pay the fee he demanded.

I didn't figure Albuquerque would pay me a fee either, so I also decided not to run through there. Actually, my reason for avoiding Albuquerque was that for approximately 100 miles east of there, Route 66 is mostly non-existent, leaving I-40 as the only alternative. To avoid those long stretches on I-40, I chose to go south on Highway 314 through Los Chavez and then south-east on Highway 47 through Belen. I planned to rejoin Route 66 and the Bunion Derby in Santa Rosa.

With lessening pain came more miles these past two days, as I was able to run about 38 miles each day. The joy of the journey had returned.

6

1,000 MILES DOWN AND 2,000 TO GO

Day 26, April 22.
Highway 47, NM to Mountainair, NM – 36.0 miles.
"You're in My Space"

AFTER NOTICING THE name of this day's destination, Mountainair, I should have known what was in store for the day. The first 10 miles were flat and through a valley, but heading for the mountains. I held out hope that the road would skirt around the mountains. Those hopes were dashed when I turned east on Highway 60 and began climbing.

The "Welcome to Mountainair" sign told the story with this description: "Elevation 6,500 feet." It had been a day of climbing as I had gained almost 2,000 feet in elevation. The 36 miles seemed longer than that, and left me with a sore inside left knee.

At the end of every day's run, we looked forward to finding a camping spot and settling down to a quiet evening. Sometimes, like this day, it wasn't as easy as it might sound. After reaching Mountainair, we purchased a couple of pizzas at the Oven Brick Pizza restaurant and headed for the local RV park that we had spotted.

Surprisingly, the RV park looked full as we parked and found the office. The manager said he had one spot left and we could use it for the one night we were staying. After paying him, we found the spot and pulled the motor home into a tight spot between two trailers. We hooked up the water and electricity and were getting ready to go inside to devour the pizza when a car came screeching to a halt in front of the motor home.

A rather irate lady got out of the car and began sharply questioning us as to why we had parked in her spot. We replied that we had paid our money and the manager told us we could park there. She stormed off to the manager's office. Soon the lady and the manager were back at our site arguing in loud voices. Apparently, she had been told by someone else that she and her husband could use that site, which was next to their trailer, to park their vehicles.

Thankfully, we remained calm during the storm and told them we would solve the problem by just moving on down the road. We told the manager to go get our money and we began unhooking the water and electricity. As we were getting ready to back out of the parking space, the lady's husband arrived from working on the railroad construction crew. I thought, "If he is anything like her, this is going to get worse before it gets better." The lady was still irate as she began telling her husband about the situation. We interrupted her long enough to tell him that we were merely running across the country, we didn't want any trouble, and we were now heading on down the road. No problem, we're on our way out.

As I mentioned earlier, Proverbs 15:1 states, *"A soft answer turns away wrath."* The husband began asking questions about my run and soon was saying that he thought there was room for them to move their vehicles to give us space for the night. It took a few minutes, but he convinced us to hook back up. After all the excitement had died down, it was on to the most important thing at that moment: eating our pizza.

A little later in the evening, Jason, the couple's 13-year-old son, came over to ask about the run. We spent some time with him, telling him about the adventures of the road. We told him about some of the nice people we had met, and elected not to tell him that his mother was the rudest person we had met on the trip. However, later that evening, his mother, who two hours earlier had been so irate and rude, knocked on the door, apologized, and gave us a $20 donation for Community Care. In turn, Mom gave Jason a Community Care T-shirt and information flyer. It was a wonderful illustration of a biblical truth: God can change hearts.

I was disappointed not to find out anything about Jed Clampett while here. I assumed he was from these parts. You Beverly Hillbilly fans might remember the theme song which said Jed was a "poor Mountainair, barely kept his family fed."

Day 27, April 23.
Mountainair, NM to Encino, NM — 40.3 miles.
"In the Dumps"

THE NEXT MORNING, Jason caught us before we pulled out of the RV park and asked that I autograph the flyer we had given him. He wished me well for the remainder of the trip.

I've been working on the railroad all the live-long day. That's what it felt like to me by the end of this day. Most of the traffic was cars, pickups and large, dirt-hauling dump trucks associated with the railroad work going on in the area. The dump trucks were apparently getting dirt from somewhere on up the road and bringing it back to the Mountainair area. Though I ran 40.3 miles for the day from Mountainair, I never reached the source of the dirt. Since the roads had no shoulders and heavy traffic, I was constantly having to step to my left off the road to avoid the large trucks and then back on the road, leading to a sore Achilles tendon on the left foot.

I ran through Willard and stopped at mileage post 245, about eight miles short of Encino. These are very small towns in a very remote area. The terrain was more desert-like, with rolling hills, few trees, and nothing green. Mom wrote that "there is nothing out here — it's as bad as the Mojave Desert." If I were writing, I would have said, "There is nothing out here — it's as **good** as the Mojave Desert." However, by this point, we were looking forward to seeing green, living things.

Day 28, April 24.
Encino, NM to Pastura, NM — 40.0 miles.
"Out to Pasture"

AFTER A DUSTY, noisy day yesterday, this day was considerably quieter and more peaceful. Early in the morning I passed the rock quarry from where all the trucks were hauling dirt back to Mountainair. Traffic was noticeably less after this point. The highway eventually had a good shoulder which, coupled with a good tail wind, made the day pass by quickly.

I was enjoying a quiet, peaceful morning run when I heard the snorting of an antelope. In the field next to the road was a large herd of antelope. The one that had snorted was closer to the road and distanced from the rest of the herd. I told him that, at this time in my life, I knew what it was like to be on the outer fringe and considered a bit strange by the rest of your kind.

Upon reaching the town of Vaughn, I turned on Highway 54 to head northeast back toward Santa Rosa. I finished the run about five miles short of Pastura, a town that was listed on the map. Thinking there might actually be a town with a RV park, we drove into Pastura looking for a RV park. It was hard to know for sure when we reached Pastura, and I'm not sure why it was on the map. There was no sign for the town and there really wasn't a town, just a few houses. In keeping with the spirit of the town, we drove down a dirt road and parked for the night in a pastura.

Day 29, April 25.
Pastura, NM to Cuervo, NM — 41.0 miles.
"Kilo Joy"

HITTING A MILESTONE was the excitement for this day. At about the 13-mile mark, near mileage sign 233 on Highway 54, I reached the 1,000-mile mark. Well, I think that's where I reached the 1,000-mile mark. With all my off-road excursions, it was impossible to always get exact mileage readings each day.

We made a small 1,000-miles sign and took pictures in the middle of a desolate road in the middle of a desolate land. In our own small way, Dad, Mom, and I celebrated God's blessings and the fact that the journey had gone better than we could have imagined.

Now that I had recovered almost completely from the shin splint, any other problem seemed minor. However, blisters and a sore Achilles tendon were causing some worry. On this day, I had experimented with bandaging and taping the sore Achilles tendon. It seemed to help, as I was able to run 41 miles.

I ran through Santa Rosa and almost to the small community of Cuervo. At day's end, we drove the 14 miles back to Santa Rosa to stay in a very nice KOA campground. Ellen, the owner of the campground, was a very gracious host. Three months earlier she moved in from Mena, Arkansas, and purchased the campground. Ellen seemed genuinely interested in learning about my run. It was always a joy to share the dream with someone and see from their expression that they were identifying with the thrill of it all. She even graciously gave a $25 donation to Community Care.

I had rejoined Route 66 in Santa Rosa and by day's end had completed 1,028 miles in 29 days. By averaging 40 miles per day the last three days, I had significantly gained ground on the Bunion Derby. They had run five fewer miles in their 29 days, but were spending this same night in Newkirk, 10 miles further down the road. Though having run fewer miles, the Bunion Derby was further down the road due to a combination of my taking a different, longer route from Los Lunas and my off-road excursions — like the time I followed the railroad track in Arizona, adding about six extra miles.

Through 29 days of the Bunion Derby, Souminen had increased his lead over second place Payne to about four and one-half hours. England's Peter Gavuzzi was in third place, only about one hour behind Payne. Gavuzzi would become an integral part of the Bunion Derby. Interestingly, earlier in my run, I had received an e-mail from Andy Milroy in England, "I was a good friend of Pete Gavuzzi who ran both the 1928 and 1929 races. Hope you enjoy your run — savour every minute of it — especially the hard times — they make the best stories!"

Day 30, April 26.
Cuervo, NM to Montoya, NM — 20.5 miles.
"Weather or Not To Run"

EVENTUALLY, SNOW HAPPENS! As is true in everyday life, there are those not-so-good days that make us appreciate the good days. This was a not-so-good day right from the start.

After leaving the KOA in Santa Rosa, we drove the 14 miles back to where I had stopped the previous afternoon. Dad stopped the motor home at the starting point. I got out and Dad took off down the road as I crossed four lanes of traffic, including the center median. In jogging across the grassy median, I pulled my right Achilles tendon, which already had been sore for the past two days.

As I hobbled down the road, I was running into a very strong and very cold headwind for which I had not dressed properly. I thought, "It can't get any worse than this."

Shortly thereafter, I exited the hills and began hobbling onto a large open plain where the headwind was unimpeded. I knew Dad and Mom had gone several miles down the road. As I was freezing and hobbling, I thought, "It can't get any worse than this."

By the time I caught up to where Dad and Mom were waiting, I felt like I was suffering from hypothermia. I was shivering and could not get warm even though I was inside the warm motor home. I never was able to get completely warmed, so I put on three layers of clothes, including a Gore-Tex™ running suit and a winter coat, and resumed hobbling into the wind.

Then it started to sprinkle lightly. I thought, "Well, at least I'm not getting wet."

The wind began to blow harder, and the light sprinkle was now rain. I thought, "It can't get any worse than this."

Then the torrential rain hit, but thankfully, I had again reached the motor home where Dad was parked. Incredibly, it had taken nearly seven hours to go 20.5 miles. It normally took about nine hours to travel 40 miles.

As I sat and listened to the heavy rain pound the motor home, I thought, "No problem. I'll just wait out this rain and get in a few more miles before the end of the day. The heavy rain soon turned into big flakes of snow. We sat on the side of the road for nearly three hours before we called it a day and looked for a place to park for the night. In all my pre-run dreams, I had never imagined that I would get snowed out of miles on April 26. The snow was pretty, but the day had been awfully depressing. Plus, I had lost 14 miles to the Bunion Derby pace.

Parker Drilling employee Phil Burch must have had incredible eyes to see through the rain and snow. He later e-mailed about this day when he had flown to Phoenix, "I think I saw you out the window below. I waved, but I guess you didn't see me."

Day 31, April 27.
Montoya, NM to Tucumcari, NM — 40.0 miles.
"Let the Sun In"

WHAT A DIFFERENCE a day makes. There was no rain, no snow, and only a crosswind instead of a headwind. One thing

65

remained the same: it was cold just like many of the previous days. The sore Achilles tendon loosened up after a few miles, and I was able to run better than yesterday. Maybe a 20-mile "off" day had its advantages.

This will sound rather strange, but it was very exciting today to see trees with green leaves, green grass, and green fields. I actually noticed, and enjoyed hearing, the wind blow through the leaves on the trees. From the time we had left the West Coast a month earlier, I had run in brown desert-like conditions for much of the way. The green of Tucumcari was a noticeable difference.

After we checked into the Tucumcari KOA campground, I took a shower and noticed that, with my long hair, I was actually beginning to resemble Forrest Gump. I was attempting to trim my hair in the KOA bathroom when Dad came in and said Sarah Meyer, managing editor of the local *Quay County Sun* newspaper, was outside waiting to interview me.

When we had checked into the KOA earlier in the afternoon, the camp manager had asked Dad and Mom if we were headed home. They told him, "Yes, but very slowly." They proceeded to tell him about our cross-country voyage. He then proceeded to call Sarah to inform her of this novelty that had entered Tucumcari.

Sarah joined us in the motor home as we ate dinner, and she asked several questions about the run. She was very nice, and not once did she let her "this-guy-must-be-insane" thoughts come to the surface. I never saw her article, but hope to look it up in the archives one day.

Most people could not relate to "wanting" to run across the United States, but there were several exceptions. Scott Roark of Charleston, South Carolina could relate as he e-mailed, "You are running the run that many of us dream of. [*Editorial note: Ending a sentence in a prepositional phrase is not something I personally believe in.*] I have often mentioned this very run to friends and family and then gotten that look, 'He must be insane.' "

It was surprising how many people I had never met e-mailed me and told me that they, too, had dreamed of running across the United States. Tim Roberts wrote, "To run across the states has also been a dream of mine for a long time, and I hope to take that long run someday." Eva Andrews closed her e-mail by saying, "From another ultra-marathoner who wishes she could run across America, Eva." Franz Tockner from Austria may not have totally grasped my effort when he said in his e-mail, " I wish you the best for your race. Perhaps I will do the same race in a few years." I never heard from these folks again, but I, too, hope they get an opportunity to take that long run.

Day 32, April 28.
Tucumcari, NM to past Glenrio, TX — 38.0 miles.
"Outback Adventure"

GOING BACK IN my mind over the previous 31 days, it was hard to believe that it had been one month ago this morning that I had started at Santa Monica Beach. I had covered many more miles in one month than I had thought possible. I rejoiced as I thought about how well (and quickly) the month had gone.

After about nine miles, I reached the small town of San Jon (pronounced San Hone), where I had to choose from three different routes which a convenience store employee had explained to Mom. The north frontage road would soon end, and that left just two choices: 19 miles on old nemesis I-40, or 19 miles on an old and original section of Route 66, which had never been paved. You can guess which one I chose. Adventure and avoidance! Adventure on an isolated gravel and dirt road and avoidance of I-40 and its traffic.

I experienced a great deal of history as I saw abandoned buildings and old original railroad tracks and bridges. Best of all, only four cars went by during the 19 miles on this old, unpaved portion of Route 66. That's right, four cars passed by in

19 miles. That's even better, meaning less traffic, than the Mohave Desert section.

Little traffic was the best of this outback excursion; however, the worst was that I had rendered my crew unavailable because of the primitive road conditions. Dad stayed on I-40, which paralleled about one mile north of the old road. Having gone 19 miles on dusty roads with no liquids or food, I was shuffling on empty by the time I reached the motor home in Glenrio. Empty as in "I'm not sure how much farther I could have gone."

Glenrio is a tiny town that straddles the New Mexico/Texas state line. It was good to have another state behind me and get back to living on Tulsa time, the Central Time Zone. After a few pictures and much liquid guzzling, I sloshed on down dirt farm roads for 10 more miles before calling it a day and parking at Stuckey's, a roadside restaurant/tourist shop.

After I would finish running for the day, I lived a life of luxury due to my wonderful crew, Dad and Mom. When we arrived at Stuckey's, Mom got the ice bags ready and helped me apply them to my Achilles tendon that had a knot on it, as well as to the shin and both ankles. Dad got my next-day shoes ready and gave the sore areas a rubdown. Mom later went into Stuckey's and bought me two hamburgers, a large order of French fries and a chocolate malt. (After all that, I was eating again two hours later.) Life was great — lots of food and a laptop PC to get e-mail messages from friends and family.

While in Stuckey's, Mom met Wyatt King, a 10th grader who worked there. She told him about my run. On his break, he came out to the motor home. We had a wonderful visit as he told us about running cross-country and track and playing basketball for his high school team. Isn't it true in life that whatever events may take place in our lives, it's the people that we meet and get to know that make them so memorable?

Day 33, April 29.
Past Glenrio, TX to Wildorado, TX — 40.0 miles.
"Not Having a Blast"

AFTER A FOUR-MILE stint on I-40 early in the morning, the rest of the run was on old Route 66, which runs adjacent to I-40. I listened to the trucks roar by all day, but I didn't have to bear the wind blasts that come from running on the shoulder. I passed some time by counting the number of semi-trucks that passed by. *[There's that darn preposition at the end of the sentence again!]* During one mile of running, 40 semis rushed by from east to west; and that didn't include several RVs, moving vans, and busses. If I had been on I-40 instead of adjacent Route 66, a large vehicle would have blasted by on average about every 35 yards. I was thankful to be on the narrow two-lane road with little traffic.

I ran through the small towns of Adrian, the self-proclaimed mid-point of Route 66 between Los Angeles and Chicago, and Vega. I had a pacer as we finished in the small town of Wildorado. Dad ran the last 13 miles with me. At the age of 68, he still was an accomplished runner, winning his age bracket in many local races.

The landscape is open and almost totally flat. It makes for easier running, but the flat does have its drawbacks. I could see the grain elevators of Wildorado eight miles before I got there; it seemed to take forever to get to the finish.

On the Bunion Derby's 33rd day, they ran from Vega to Amarillo and had completed 1,175 miles compared to my 1,166 miles for the same number of days. My 20.5-mile snow-out day had dropped me behind their pace. However, their snow day had come on this, the 33rd day. It had snowed during the first half of their 37-mile run and then turned to rain. Three days ago, my day had been just the opposite: rain followed by snow. At this point in the race, Souminen had stretched his lead to more than five hours over Payne and Gavuzzi.

For me, it was "Amarillo by morning," as the song goes.

Day 34, April 30.
Wildorado, TX to Amarillo Exit 85, TX — 38.0 miles.
"Abridged Edition"

"VAST" SEEMED LIKE the best description of Amarillo. Not only was it Amarillo by morning, but it was Amarillo by noon and Amarillo by evening. It seemed to take all day to get across the large metropolitan area. The city limits sign stated it had a population of 168,000. That may not be much compared to large cities, but if I added the population of every town in New Mexico and Texas that I had run through thus far, it wouldn't add up to that much.

Unfortunately, I arrived in downtown Amarillo right at noon, and there was much activity on the sidewalks. After all the days of being in wide-open spaces, I felt very conspicuous and out of place negotiating the busy sidewalks and streets.

At one location near the downtown area, the old Route 66 goes over an overpass. At this point, there is no sidewalk on the bridge, only three narrow lanes going one way toward me. As I started over the overpass, there were no cars coming. As I neared the middle of the bridge, a string of cars in all three lanes came over the rise toward me. Have you ever felt like a trapped rat with nowhere to go and nowhere to hide? All I could do was hug the sides, pray, and keep making progress toward the other side.

As quickly as possible, I got across the bridge unharmed and was thankful to eventually reach the far side of Amarillo and call it a day. We camped at a RV park near the airport. It was warm enough that we could sit outside and enjoy watching a B-1 bomber practice touch-and-go landings.

It had been a difficult day in that I hadn't felt well and the Achilles tendon had been inflamed and swollen the past few days. Dad and Mom had tried to call Dr. Hendrix in Tulsa in order to obtain some more anti-inflammatory medicine, but they had not been able to contact him. I followed the advice of a local pharmacist who recommended taking extra Ibuprofen, which seemed to help reduce the swelling.

Day 35, May 1.
Amarillo Exit 85, TX to Exit 124, TX — 39.5 miles.
"Well Groomed"

ENDING APRIL AND beginning May — it was a new month! I ran through Conway and on to Groom where I received a wonderful surprise. Actually, it wasn't a total surprise; word had leaked out in an e-mail. However, I was so delighted, it was easy to act surprised. For the past two weeks, we had planned for my brother Wayne and his special son Ryan to drive up from his then hometown of Fort Worth and relieve my parents for three days.

However, before Wayne and Ryan arrived, Marcy and our good friend Eric Freeman "surprised me" by showing up as I was running through Groom. It had been nearly five weeks since I had seen my wife, and it was a tremendous thrill to see her again. Though I was still many miles from the halfway point, it suddenly seemed as though the hard part was finished. I had been able to overcome most of the nagging injuries that I had battled since the start, and I was certainly in much better overall condition than when I had started nearly five weeks ago. Sharing three days with Marcy — life was really good right now.

We took a few pictures at the leaning water tower in Groom, Texas. If you're ever traveling through west Texas on I-40, watch for the tower just to the north of the highway — if it's still standing, that is. After the pictures had been taken, Dad and Mom headed home in Marcy's car for a well-deserved break from the road and all the work that the crew did. By their diary entries,

71

they must have been quite excited to escape the motor home and go home to see family and friends.

Eric accompanied me the last few miles on a bicycle that we had strapped on the motor home, but had never used. We finished the day's run at Exit 124 on I-40 and drove to Lake McClellan State Park, where we enjoyed a beautiful evening by having a cookout and catching up on the past five weeks. Not only had it been a dramatic 35th day for me, but also for Andy Payne.

A significant development took place on the 35th day of the Bunion Derby. Leader Arne Souminen pulled an Achilles tendon (do you think he, too, had just gotten out of a motor home and was running across a grassy median?) just after the start in Groom, Texas. He managed to hobble the remaining miles and finish the 38.8-mile segment over three hours behind Payne. However, Souminen would not be able to start the following day, thus dropping from the race. Payne was back in the overall lead, leading Gavuzzi by over two hours.

Day 36, May 2.
Exit 124, TX to Shamrock, TX — 39.0 miles.
"Homeward Bound"

TODAY'S MEMORY VERSE seemed particularly appropriate. Psalm 121:1-2: *"I will lift up my eyes to the hills, from whence comes my help. My help comes from the Lord."* The first half of the day's run included canyons and more hills than I had seen in the previous three days. We also saw several deer before we even left the state park in the early morning.

I ran through Alanreed and took a lunch break at the Route 66 Museum in McLean. All of us toured the museum, which was loaded with Route 66 memorabilia and history. It's a recommended place to visit if you get the opportunity. McLean is also home of the first Phillips 66 station in Texas, which had been restored and provided an occasion for more pictures.

My crew bought a Route 66 car tag and put it on the motor home. They also hung in the motor home window the Sapulpa Centennial banner that I had received at my send-off. We now had an official Route 66, transcontinental crew vehicle.

Later in the afternoon I came around a bend and found my crew (Marcy, Wayne, Ryan, and Eric) sitting in the shade in lawn chairs with their feet propped up. Who said this crewing was hard work? Marcy noted that I was on the final leg (no pun intended) of my run for the day. We were all ready to call it a day, which we did when we reached the U Drop Inn Café in Shamrock. Seriously, that's the name.

After feasting at the Pizza Hut, I spent the night in a hotel room — at the Best Western in Shamrock. This was the first night I had stayed in a hotel during the run. Wayne, Ryan, and Eric stayed in the motor home while Marcy and I took the hotel room. Hey, what are good friends for? I mean, "For what are good friends?" Those ending prepositions don't always go away easily. Anyhow, the guys' thoughtfulness was much appreciated.

Tomorrow: OOOOOOOOklahoma where the wind comes sweeping down the plain. I'm hoping it sweeps across the plain from the west. The last half of today was unusual in that the strong wind was coming from the northeast, which made for somewhat of a head wind. That may be why Eric decided not to accompany me on the bike today.

I really enjoyed hearing that children would get involved and caught up in the excitement of my run. Rhonda Peeples wrote, "I love reading your day-to-day updates. I print them out and take them home so my kids can keep up on your run as well. They think it is the neatest thing that you took off to run across the U.S. and that it was your dream."

Several people mentioned that their children enjoyed following my progress on maps they had at their house. I received e-mails from several classes at different schools from around

Randy entering his home state of Oklahoma.

my home area as they followed my progress by reading my website postings. Rick White, whom I was later to meet in Oklahoma, said in one of his e-mails that his children, Megan and Matthew, "have added your name to their bedtime prayers."

7

LIVING ON TULSA TIME

Day 37, May 3.
Shamrock, TX to Sayre, OK — 39.0 miles.
"In the Cards"

HOOPLA — NOT A normal happening. Most days on the road were rather uneventful. However, this one seemed eventful as several memories stand out.

Early in the morning, while running a short stretch on I-40, I noticed some football cards scattered along the grass just off the highway. Over a stretch of several hundred yards, the "some football cards" turned out to be thousands of cards. The five of us spent at least 20 minutes picking up cards and wondering what the story was behind the cards scattered alongside the road. We narrowed it down to two theories: either someone was moving and a box blew out of the back of a truck, or someone's wife had just gotten even by throwing her husband's prized card collection out the window. Either way, we collected a large cache of football cards.

After 14 miles, I reached the Oklahoma state line and the tiny town of Texola. Tricky name, huh — combining parts of

Texas and Oklahoma. It seemed as though I had come back home, although I was still 275 miles from my hometown. Now that I was back in my home state, I felt as though everyone was my friend and neighbor. It didn't take long to realize that my feelings weren't shared by the drivers, who viewed me just as strangely as had the drivers in the previous four states.

After our customary state line picture-taking session, we drove into Erick, Oklahoma, and attended worship at First Baptist Church. During the service, the song leader introduced a girl who sang a solo, a girl who looked to be about 13 years of age. She looked very nervous as she walked up on the stage. She opened her hymnal and, accompanied by her grandmother on the piano, she began to sing "Amazing Grace."

The young girl made it through the first verse just fine, never looking at her opened hymnal. During the second verse, she appeared to look down at her peers who were sitting on the first two rows. As most of us can relate, she blanked out, started to stammer, and had to quickly look at her hymnal. Probably unknowingly, she resumed with the last part of the third verse. She had started in the second verse and ended with the third verse. She composed herself and courageously sang the fourth verse. She had a good voice, but, most of all, I was impressed with her courage to get up there and then to finish the song.

After the service was finished, I approached her and told her I was from out of town and that I had really been blessed by her song. Her grandparents were standing there beaming as other people were also complimenting her. Her proud grandmother said, "This is the first time she has sung a solo."

I could really identify with her and the fear she must have had when she took the stage. She had shown true courage, courage in doing the right thing when it is the most difficult thing to do at that moment.

A few days later, I was telling the story at a school in Claremore, Oklahoma, and one of the most amazing incidents of my voyage took place. However, I'm getting ahead of myself; you will have to wait until we get to Claremore before I divulge that story. Of course, you will be able to read there faster than I was able to run there.

After church in Erick, we ate lunch at Cal's Restaurant, a famous restaurant in that neck of the woods — as they would say there. It was a delicious meal. Though I don't remember exactly what I ate, I do know that I ate way too much for someone who was planning on running all afternoon. Only a few minutes after eating, it was back on the road — on the hottest day since I had started back in late March. After about seven post-lunch miles, I felt terrible. Lunch couldn't decide whether to stay down or not.

As I was lounging in a lawn chair under a shade tree and agonizing in a state of semi-consciousness, I heard a commotion in front of the motor home. Wayne and Eric were talking to someone who had stopped alongside the desolate road that we were traveling. It sounded serious until Wayne burst out laughing.

My long-distance running friends, Jack and Brenda Christian, had driven from their home near Elk City to see if they could find us. Jack and I had run a few ultra-marathon races together. I say "ran together," but, actually, I never could stay up with him. He has been, and continues to be, an outstanding long-distance runner.

With the arrival of Jack and Brenda, and the application of a few more cold, wet towels, I felt much better. Jack joined me as we ran nine more miles into Sayre, where Wayne, Ryan, and I spent the night in the motor home in the Sayre City Park. Marcy and Eric had headed home earlier on this Sunday afternoon. It was hard to say good-bye to Marcy, but I knew I was getting closer to home and I would see her again in a few days.

After this day's run, I had caught back up to the Bunion Derby pace. Amazingly, both the Bunion Derby runners and I stayed all night in Sayre after 37 days of running. Even more amazing, my log showed that our mileage totals were only three-tenths of a mile different, both about 1,322 miles.

On this day in the Bunion Derby, Oklahoma had joyously welcomed home its native son. Many Oklahoma newspapers carried front-page pictures and articles about the Bunion Derby and its leader, Oklahoma's own Andy Payne.

That night, I sat and imagined all the excitement and crowds 70 years ago. As old as the Sayre City Park seemed, and with its location right next to downtown, I could envision our motor home being parked right in the middle of the Bunion Derby entourage. Come to think of it, the restroom and shower facility in the park was so old, it also may have been used by the Bunion Derby runners.

Day 38, May 4.
Sayre, OK to Clinton, OK — 39.8 miles.
"Onward, Christian Runner"

IN THE EARLY morning, Jack Christian rejoined me and ran the entire 39.8 miles with me. With his company, the day seemed to go by very quickly.

As was my Monday custom, I called John Erling, disk jockey (make that "radio personality") at Tulsa radio station KRMG, for a live update before I started running in the morning. Jack's wife, Brenda, had also arranged for me to stop by radio station KECO as I ran through Elk City. When Jack and I reached Elk City, we ran a few blocks off Route 66 and located the radio station.

The morning personalities at KECO were John Tracy and Jim King, who is called "King of the Road" because he regularly gives Route 66 trivia. The live interview seemed to go all right until one of Jim's questions. He surprised me by asking, "Now, you can tell me the truth, do you sometimes take rides?" To me, it was inconceivable even to consider such a thing. Why would a person dream for years about running across the country and then take short-cuts so that he could not honestly say he completed the full journey? The interview ended shortly after that question and I was back on the road.

A few minutes later as Jack and I were running through Elk City, a man suddenly appeared fifty yards ahead of us pointing something at us. We cautiously approached and discovered that he was a reporter taking pictures for the local newspaper. After an "on-the-street" interview, Jack and I were back at it.

Also in Elk City, we ran by a strange site, a large drilling rig set up next to the road. It was then that I remembered that several years ago, Parker Drilling Company, my former employer, had donated its Rig 114 to the town of Elk City. Parker had set up the rig so Elk City could use it as a museum.

Dad and Mom left Sapulpa early in the morning and drove three hours west to rejoin us at about 9:30 a.m. Wayne and Ryan had been a wonderful crew for three days, but now had to return to Fort Worth to the real world.

Jack and I ran through the small towns of Canute and Foss and ended the run about five miles west of Clinton. All during the day, Jack and I talked much about the Bunion Derby, which had run along these same roads 70 years before us. Jack often passed the time by making comments like, "I bet Andy Payne stopped in that old café," and, "Which side of this road do you think Andy Payne ran on?" I then understood what my family had listened to from me for the previous five years. After many days of solitary running, it was enjoyable having someone with whom to share my Bunion Derby dream as we ran along and visited together.

Day 39, May 5.
Clinton, OK to Bridgeport, OK — 38.0 miles.
"For Whom the Bell Tolls"

STROLLING THROUGH CLINTON, I experienced a peaceful early morning run as I enjoyed its green parks, ball fields, and golf course. The church bells were playing the old hymn, "Crown Him Lord of All," on this Tuesday morning. Though not the case, I imagined that they were playing that great old hymn just for my enjoyment as I passed through the town.

However, it didn't take long to get back to the reality of the task at hand. A strong head wind, high humidity, and warm temperatures made for a long, struggling day. That, coupled with heavier-than-usual traffic on shoulderless old Route 66, made for many road step-offs and step-ons. Dad was able to "enjoy" the headwind by running with me for about ten miles in the morning.

After running through Weatherford, I soon discovered the reason for the extra traffic: a large auction outside of Hydro. This must have been a major local production. There were cars parked on the side of the road for nearly a mile, which caused a great deal of congestion for me to negotiate. What's the deal? Didn't they know that they are clogging up my own personal running route? They didn't seem to notice or care.

After 37.5 miles, and about six miles short of Bridgeport, I had run out of gas. After the high enthusiasm of running with Jack the previous day (at probably too fast a pace), I struggled on this day.

We drove into the small community of Bridgeport and parked in a driveway next to a vacant house. Mom cooked a wonderful meal of charcoal steaks, baked potatoes (is that "e" supposed to be in there?), carrots, and bread. As though second helpings weren't enough, I topped it off with a large helping of chocolate ice cream. I ate so much that I didn't eat again for two whole hours. During the few weeks of my journey, I would have matched my appetite against any of those Sumo wrestlers you see on television.

Our peaceful evening was interrupted shortly before dinner when the owners of the vacant house, that we were parked by, stopped and questioned us. The house had been broken into a few days earlier, and the owners thought the thieves might be back — as though the thieves would park a motor home by the targeted house and charcoal steaks on an outside grill. After a few moments of explanation on our part, everything was fine and they allowed us to stay there. However, I wouldn't be surprised if they didn't drive by a couple of more times that evening to check on us. Being out in the middle of a rural area and our story of running across the country — how credible or believable would that seem to the locals?

Day 40, May 6.
Bridgeport, OK to Yukon, OK — 39.8 miles.
"Ride the Pony"

THIS MORNING PROVIDED some of my favorite running conditions. The temperature was about 60 degrees with a dense fog, reducing visibility to about 50 yards for the first few miles of the day. As I plodded down Route 66, I was in my own little cocoon, a cocoon that seemingly moved down the road with me.

I enjoyed the waving wheat fields and the streams surrounded with thick groves of trees, water dripping from their leaves. Chirping birds serenaded me as I took in the beauty of God's creation. My clothes were soaking up the moisture of the air as I soaked up priceless memories of a peaceful morning run near Bridgeport, Oklahoma.

Shortly after Bridgeport was the narrow 4,000-foot-long Pony Bridge built in 1933 over the Canadian River. It was very narrow, barely enough room for two cars to pass. As I was scurrying across the bridge, a large truck, carrying pipe, came from one direction, and a passenger car came from the other direction. Neither driver slowed down, and it was soon evident they were going to pass at the spot where I was running, or had been running. I literally climbed the iron railing on the side of the bridge to narrowly escape being thrown from the Pony. It was with a tremendous sense of relief that I finally reached the other end of the bridge. They don't make them like they used to, and aren't we glad when it comes to bridges.

I ran through El Reno and reached Yukon by the end of the run. Marcy's cousin, Glenda, and her daughter, Christy, met us there and accompanied us to Marcy's Aunt Thetis' house to park the motor home for the night. After many nights of solitude on the roads, it was nice to enjoy the hospitality and home cooking of relatives. Additionally, it was always comforting to park the motor home in a safe place versus off to the side of the road in remote areas.

We had an exciting phone call from Wayne, my crew leader, last weekend. He accepted a job in Tulsa, and he and his family would be leaving Fort Worth and moving back to Sapulpa. Dad and Mom were excited: more grandchildren living in the same town with them.

For you country and western fans, Garth Brooks is a native of Yukon, Oklahoma. I just assumed that he and his family would be there to welcome us, but we never saw him. He must not have gotten the message that we were coming through town.

Day 41, May 7.
Yukon, OK to Arcadia Lake, OK — 39.0 miles.
"Capitolizing on Prayer"

OSCILLATING BETWEEN THE current and the old, I enjoyed a day of recalling some of my early adulthood memories. Additionally, in contrast to the many hours of running alone in desolate areas, this was the most sociable day of the journey.

At about the nine-mile mark, I reached Lake Overholser on the northwest side of Oklahoma City. In my college days, it was known as Lake "Hold 'er closer" — but that's another story. I looked forward to reaching this section because the Andy Payne Memorial Marathon course runs around this lake. This is the race where I first learned about Andy Payne and the Bunion

Derby. In a sense, this was the birthplace of the cross-country run I was doing. As the race director points out each year, the Bunion Derby had run across the old iron bridge still being used at the north end of the lake.

As I reached the memorable bridge, there were three people waiting to meet me: Oklahoma City Running Club president, Sam Loy, and members, Jim Roblyer and Jim Smith. They graciously welcomed me to Oklahoma City and presented my parents and me with running club bandanas.

As I left the lake and headed toward the state capitol, I reminisced on the memories of having lived for awhile in this area. I ran by the school where Marcy, my fiancée at that time, had interviewed for her first teaching job. Later, I ran by the small and very modest apartments across the street from Oklahoma City University where we had lived when we were first married. Upon thinking of the early years of our marriage, I was filled with gratitude for how God had blessed us over the years.

When I reached the state capitol at noon, there were many people and much commotion. I thought, "All this for me?" Actually, it was better than a welcoming committee; it was a celebration to commemorate the national day of prayer. I must have looked out of place in my running attire, but I joined right in and enjoyed the festivities. In addition, some more Oklahoma City Running Club members were there and gave me a club hat and shirt. Glenda and Christy brought a picnic lunch, which we enjoyed on the capitol grounds.

Then it was on to the Oklahoma City suburb of Edmond where Marcy and I had gone to college and had lived for a few years. This was a day that could be called a "running club" day. When I reached Edmond, the Edmond Running Club president, Jeff Blackwell, joined me for the eight miles of running through Edmond and to the I-35 crossing. Also joining me for this portion was Wayne's son, Daniel, an outstanding track and cross-country runner. He had flown to Oklahoma City from Fort Worth, and Dad and Mom picked him up at the airport. Running past Marcy's and my old alma mater in Edmond, the University of Central Oklahoma, brought back a flood of wonderful memories. As I was nearing the end of the day's run, I was honored when Oklahoma long-distance running legend, Harry Deupree, found me to say hello. Harry had been an inspiration to me in my earlier days of running ultra-distance races. He had completed more ultra-distance races than one can imagine, including several 100-mile races in the high mountains of Leadville, Colorado. He was known to long-distance runners all over the country for his endurance, friendliness, and graceful running style. Harry wished me well and gave me a small Bible that I will always treasure.

We finished at the Arcadia Lake Park entrance and camped there for the night. The Edmond Running Club paid the park fee, and Jeff returned with a club running shirt for me, as well as some much-needed bags of ice. No telling how many bags of ice we used on the run, mostly for applying to my legs, shins, ankles, and knees. Later in the evening, running club members, Vaughn DeWolfe and Rick and Lori White, with children Megan and Matthew, drove out to the lake and joined us for a pleasant evening. We had never met these folks, but it was enjoyable to get to know them and share the road stories with them.

While I had a dozen or so people welcome me to the Oklahoma City/Edmond area, Andy Payne had several thousands of people welcome him. The Bunion Derby runners finished their 41st day at the Oklahoma City Fairgrounds, as the largest crowds of the race lined the streets to see the runners. Payne had a one-and-a-half-hour lead over Peter Gavuzzi. Payne's race strategy was set: stay with Gavuzzi all day and don't let him reduce the overall lead.

Although I was 15 miles further down the road after 41 days, my running log only showed me having run two miles more than the Bunion Derby at this point. I had no idea at the time, but during this day I had reached the halfway point of my cross-country run.

Day 42, May 8.
Arcadia Lake, OK to Davenport, OK — 39.5 miles.
"Memory Lane"

NEGOTIATING THROUGH THE campground early in the morning, I resumed running on old Route 66 at the park's entrance and was soon joined by two local runners. Running with others generally provided a welcomed break and enjoyable conversation. However, it was not so enjoyable this time.

In addition to the heavy traffic heading to work, the old road had no shoulder, which was not conducive to running together. That, coupled with a headwind and drivers reluctant to share the road, made for a tough start.

There's a certain misconception that many people, especially runners, had about me. The misconception was this: I must be this super runner who can run really fast since I run such long distances. In reality, it's generally just the opposite. The longer distances one runs, the slower he usually runs. Speed and distance are a lethal combination for everyone except the very elite, world-class long-distance runners. I'm slow!

One of the runners accompanying me on this morning must have had that misconception right from the start. After a few moments of running my pace, he would take the lead and then proceed to run faster than me, getting 50 or so yards ahead and then having to wait for me. He could never "idle down" to my pace.

I think he must have been disappointed to realize that I was very ordinary and plodded along at a 9-to-10-minute-per-mile pace. I couldn't help thinking, "You're only going four miles this morning; if you were to run with me all day, at three o'clock in the afternoon you wouldn't be sprinting ahead and waiting for me. I'd be waiting for you."

Other than the first few miles of heavy traffic, it was an enjoyable day as I relived one of the most memorable days of my life — one that took place on these roads 24 years ago almost to the very day. I had taken my last final test for the spring semester at college in 1974. The next morning, I got up early and proceeded to undertake my first long-distance run. A friend had bet me that I couldn't run/walk the 50 miles from Edmond to Stroud in less than 15 hours.

I had done little training, wore a pair of thin-soled tennis shoes, used no sun block, and carried a canteen. All of those are not good things when it comes to long-distance running. I did make the 50 miles in 13 hours, but I looked like a half-dead, half-cooked red lobster when Mom picked me up in downtown Stroud. I could hardly walk for days afterward.

I never cashed my friend's check that I won on the bet. I figured the paper memorabilia was worth more than the $15 that I had nearly killed myself to win. That was certainly a difficult debut to my long-distance running career. Compared to that day, the 39.5 miles on this day was a walk in the park. Isn't that incredible: 22 years young then versus 46 years old this day; well rested then versus having done 39 miles the day previous to this one — and, yet, this day was a piece of cake compared to the misery of that day 24 years ago. All I can say is that training and know-how make a tremendous difference.

On this day, I ran through the small Route 66 towns of Arcadia, Luther, Wellston, Warwick, Chandler, and ended in Davenport. In the morning, Dad and Mom drove the motor home 80 miles to their house for a few days' break. Marcy rejoined me in our van to provide support — the essentials, water and food.

We stopped at the Chandler Historical Museum and viewed Bunion Derby pictures from when the race had come through Chandler. The museum also had an original, official race program that was sold when the race came through town. I was able to make a copy of the program, which contains race information and bios on all the race entrants.

On this, the 42nd day of the Bunion Derby, the runners had finished in Chandler. Gavuzzi had run the 51.9 miles from Oklahoma City in an incredible 7 hours, 54 minutes. Payne had finished just over an hour behind him, resulting in Payne's lead being reduced to 30 minutes. This had set up an epic battle as they neared Tulsa and Payne's hometown of Foyil.

For only the second time in 42 days, we stayed in a hotel room for the night, this time in Stroud. We ate at the Route 66 Rock Café. Marcy hadn't been with me very much and she was astonished at my appetite. Dinner for me included a large plate of spaghetti with Texas toast and a large double cheeseburger, plus finishing off a significant portion of Marcy's french fries and brisket. One and one-half hours later, I was eating pretzels in the hotel room. She had never seen metabolism like this! I tell you, I could have challenged those Sumo wrestlers – on eating or running, not wrestling.

Day 43, May 9.
Davenport, OK to Kellyville, OK — 37.0 miles.
"Self Swerving"

LICKING MY FINGERS after I finished the last chocolate donut, I thought, "I have eaten two bagels, two pancakes and a potato cake from McDonald's, several peanut butter crackers, a chocolate long john, and two chocolate donuts — and it isn't yet 8:30 a.m. It's just another ordinary day on the road.

Earlier in the morning, Marcy drove me back to Davenport where I began the day. I ran through Stroud and then, nearing Depew, I realized that, yes, I was back home in Oklahoma. I could see it coming from the west and it quickly overtook us — a severe thunderstorm. Marcy and I sat in the van for 20 minutes listening to KRMG's storm reports and waiting out the worst of the storm. It brought back memories from New Mexico where I had sat in the motor home for hours waiting for a storm to pass. However, this one went quickly and I was soon back running after the rain subsided and the lightning passed.

About two miles before reaching Bristow, a van that was coming toward me suddenly veered off the road just a few yards in front of me. Fortunately, I didn't make any wild gestures, because it was good friends David and Marsha Pritz and our Pastor Roy Emmons and his wife Norma. They had driven 30 miles from our hometown to welcome me back. It was sure good to see friends that I hadn't seen in over six weeks. After a few minutes of greeting, I ran on into Bristow and joined them and Marcy for lunch at the Tastee Freeze diner.

I was now close enough to home that I would sleep in my own bed this night — and see my children, Heather 19, Justin 16, and Nicole 13, for the first time since leaving on March 25. I finished my run four miles west of Kellyville at the Polecat Creek Bridge. Yes, we have a creek by that name in our area. I've lived here most of my life and still don't know what a polecat is.

We drove the 15 miles to my house, and I was able to clean up and get to Nicole's soccer game in time to see her post a shut-out as the goalie. The fact that most of the game was played in a pouring rain didn't faze a dad who had run 1,554 miles just to get there in the nick of time. I'm positive that I would have won the "came from the farthest away" award.

Ahhh! A night at home. It was wonderful!!!

Day 44, May 10.
0 miles.
"Home On the Range"

YEAH! AFTER 43 days, the Bunion Derby had spent the night in Bristow back down the road 15 miles. I had managed to catch up again and was just ahead of their pace. On day 43, Gavuzzi had managed to again finish nearly one hour ahead of Payne. Therefore, as the runners camped at Bristow's City Park, the race had a new leader; England's Peter Gavuzzi now led Payne by nearly 30 minutes.

This was Sunday and Mother's Day. Before the run, I had never dreamed that I would be back home on Mother's Day. I was several days ahead of where I anticipated I would be on this date. I had been extremely blessed, and this day worked out perfectly.

I was able to attend Sapulpa Bible Church, my home church, and just enjoy a relaxing day. They asked me to speak during church and share about my journey thus far. After 52 years, I still have not accepted very well the fact that I'm a rather emotional person. Trying to relate the thrill of the first six weeks, coupled with the emotions of being home for a couple of days, made speaking to my home congregation harder than I had anticipated. I, for one, would consider a tear duct vasectomy, if there were such a thing.

The one concern I had about staying at my house and sleeping in my own bed was whether it would be difficult to leave and resume the journey. Several people asked whether it was risky staying in my own house for a few days. Oddly enough, this would prove not to be a problem. I was ready and anxious to head east and complete the dream.

Day 45, May 11.
Kellyville, OK to Sapulpa, OK — 13.0 miles.
"Escort Service"

THIS WAS THE shortest run, yet the most exciting day. I was only going to run the 13 miles it would take to reach my home-town of Sapulpa. For most of my life, I never thought of 13 miles being a short afternoon jog.

I started the day by visiting and speaking to students at three different schools in Sapulpa: Faith Central Christian School, Washington Elementary and the school district where we live, Pretty Water School. It was enjoyable sharing the trip with all these students and fielding their questions. Next on the day's schedule was a lunch-time visit to Parker Drilling Company, my former employer. I also squeezed in a haircut to ward off some of the Forrest Gump comparisons.

After a day of socializing, it was difficult to leave friends and head back to the road to resume running. Marcy drove me back to the Polecat Creek Bridge so that I could run in to Sapulpa. It was a thrill to run on some of the original concrete pavement of Route 66, the portion of roads on which I had trained. Friend Laddie Ondracek joined me for this segment of the run.

Just west of Sapulpa, I stopped by Mr. and Mrs. Frank Smeltzer's house and had strawberry shortcake with them. I had met Mr. Smeltzer on one of my Saturday morning training runs several months earlier. His dad had bought the house in which he was living in the early 1920s. Mr. Smeltzer was 11 years old in 1928 when he watched the Bunion Derby runners and their entourage pass by his house. I always enjoyed him sharing his memories of the race.

After the dessert, I ran to the VFW building on the west side of Sapulpa. Waiting for me were several Sapulpa High School cross-country and track runners, plus several other runners from the area and Tulsa Running Club. We had a police escort as we ran the two miles into downtown Sapulpa. One of the moments I will never forget is when we topped the hill west of Sapulpa and saw downtown Sapulpa. It was good to be home!

Waiting at the downtown gazebo were many friends to welcome me home. I was honored and humbled to be greeted by so many friends, including Mayor Brian Bingman. We ate hamburgers and hot dogs as a fundraiser for Community Care. The Pretty Water choir had joined the festivities and sang "One Small Step." I don't remember what I said to the crowd, but I know I was filled with gratitude and wanted to convey my appreciation for their encouragement and prayers. We rushed from there to Pretty Water School and enjoyed my daughter Nicole's flute recital.

Wow! That was a whole bunch of activity to cram into one day. It had been an exciting and thrilling day, one that could only be topped by reaching the finish line, God willing.

Being interviewed by an Oklahoma City television station.

8

RAN OUT OF TOWN

Day 46, May 12.
Sapulpa, OK to Catoosa, OK — 35.5 miles.
"Payneful School Memories"

SURPRISE! WHEN I arrived at the downtown gazebo in the early morning to resume my run, there were 14 Tulsa Running Club members there to run a few miles with Dad and me. After we ran about seven miles into the edge of Tulsa, the crowd was gone and it was back to running by myself. I did have an occasional fan cheering for me, as Marcy's mother, Betty Smith, her sister Esther and son Russell John drove by to say hello.

A teacher at the Eugene Field Elementary School had found out about my run and my website. Since the school was only about one block from Route 66, he had e-mailed me and asked if I would come by the school. I had agreed to, but told him I wasn't sure exactly what time I would get there.

He must have sent out a spotter to locate me. By the time I got there, there were hundreds of students outside waiting for me on the playground, pressed against the chain link fence with signs and loud cheers. It was exciting to share with them for just five minutes or so. I will never forget the cheers and good wishes from those students.

Near downtown Tulsa, the old Route 66 crossed the Arkansas River over a long bridge. The old original bridge has now been barricaded, with large chain-link fences installed on each end. Knowing the Bunion Derby runners had run over that very bridge, I was determined to do likewise. I was able to squeeze through a small hole in the fencing and run across the bridge. I could vividly imagine Andy Payne running across the bridge and looking at the large downtown buildings just blocks away. Of course, Andy Payne didn't have to hunt for another small hole to crawl through when he reached the other end of the bridge.

On April 16, 1928, the Bunion Derby runners had started in Bristow and had run 41.7 miles to Lee School, now Lee Elementary, on the south side of downtown Tulsa. The runners had finished in the football stadium at the school and had slept inside the auditorium at the school. Lee Elementary was built in 1922 and provided spacious room for the runners to stay inside. Gavuzzi had again finished ahead of Payne, this time by nearly 45 minutes. Was Gavuzzi pulling away from Payne right in the heart of Payne's home state?

Susan Oldham, a physical education teacher at Lee Elementary, was a former neighbor of ours. She had e-mailed me and asked if I would stop by the school on my run. No one will ever understand the thrill it was for me to stand in the middle of that same auditorium and tell 100 students the Andy Payne story. They were sitting on the floor in the very same spots where those runners had slept 70 years earlier. I'm sure I was more energized than at any other time I spoke, but the students seemed captivated and full of wonder as we imagined together what it was like on those grounds in 1928.

After a wonderful hour at the school, I left and ran down Tulsa's 11th Street, the old Route 66 road. The rest of the day could not be anything but anti-climatic as I struggled to finish out a 35-mile day in hot weather. I had talked Marcy into taking time off from her crewing job; therefore, I was on my own for most of the day. It was one of the hottest days, and I was stopping at convenience stores, food shops, and pop machines trying to get enough liquids and food. It made me realize how helpful it had been to have Dad and Mom meeting me every few miles in the motor home.

I finished my day by the old iron bridge on Route 66 east of Catoosa, where Marcy had trouble finding me at day's end. Some of the old Route 66 sections can be difficult to locate in certain areas. Once she found and rescued me from fatigue and heat, we were heading the 25 miles back home for the next-to-last night spent at home.

Since he was not having to be the crew on this day, Dad spent some of the day getting new tires put on the motor home and doing minor repairs and maintenance. Old Daisy had done well during the first half; it certainly had fewer ailments than I did. We were praying it, and me, would hold up on the second half as well as we had on the first half.

Day 47, May 13.
Catoosa, OK to Chelsea, OK — 36.0 miles.
"Filled to the Brim"

ON THE ROAD again. Early in the morning, Marcy and I loaded our van with supplies, food, and liquids, and headed back to Catoosa. After I resumed the day at the old iron bridge outside of Catoosa, a friend and outstanding local runner, Ray Lattanzia, joined me for a few of the early miles. A few days earlier I had received an e-mail from teacher Janice Brim inviting me to speak at First Baptist Christian School when I ran through Claremore. Upon reaching Claremore, I detoured about a mile off Route 66 and stopped by the school.

95

I doubt whether they had ever had a chapel speaker come into the church auditorium dressed in running attire — perspiration-laden running attire at that. It was wonderful to share both Andy Payne's story and my story to an attentive and thoughtful group of approximately 200 students. They even took up an offering at the end of my talk to give to Community Care. Now, to divulge one of the most incredible things that happened on the whole run. When I spoke to the students in Claremore, I told about the incident in Erick, Oklahoma.

You may recall that on Day 37 I had written about attending church in Erick, where a young, very nervous girl sang "Amazing Grace," her first solo. I used that as an example to the students about having the courage to do the right thing even if it might be the most difficult thing to do at that time. I sometimes was asked, "Does it take a lot of courage to run across the country?" I emphasized that courage is not running across the country and doing what a person really enjoys doing, but courage is doing the right thing when it's difficult and not what you want to do at that time. After I told the students the story of the young vocalist, I ended by saying that I wish I had gotten that girl's name in Erick, Oklahoma. I enjoyed using her as an example of courage, but I always regretted not remembering her name.

After I finished speaking to the students, Janice came up to me and asked, "Did you say that you heard that girl at First Baptist Church in Erick?"

After telling her yes, she said, "You're not going to believe this, but my sister, Lenita O'Neil, attends that church and plays the organ for the church. I am sure she was there that morning and I can get the girl's name from her. I'll call her and e-mail you in the next couple of days." Sure enough, I received an e-mail that night from Janice. Her sister had played the organ at church the Sunday I was there in the small church in the small town of Erick, Oklahoma.

I could hardly believe it. Think about it: I just happen to go to the one school that happens to have the one teacher who happens to have the one sister who happens to go to the one church 350 miles away that I just happened to go to ten days earlier. I have often thanked God for an "incident" that he orchestrated as a real blessing during the trip. Oh yes, the girl's name was Katie Smotherman.

After running through Claremore, it was off to a part of the run that I had looked forward to from the very first day. I reached Foyil, Oklahoma, birthplace and hometown of Andy Payne himself. Marcy and I stopped by the Andy Payne monument and took several pictures. We enjoyed meeting a few local residents and telling them about my run and sharing stories about the Bunion Derby.

As I stood on the streets of Foyil, I could just visualize the cheering crowds that lined the streets that day on April 17, 1928, as their local hero ran through town. He was battling for the overall lead with England's Peter Gavuzzi, so he could not take much time to enjoy and to talk to his hometown fans.

A few miles earlier, a large crowd, including bands and resident Will Rogers himself, had welcomed Payne as he ran into Claremore. Payne had only spoken briefly to the throng that greeted him. The race clock was ticking; he had to finish the 50-mile run into Chelsea. Payne did indeed finish first in that day's segment, covering the 50 miles in an incredible 7 hours, 23 minutes. He had gained nearly three hours on his rival Gavuzzi, thereby regaining the overall lead. The home fans had spurred him on to an amazing time that day. Had Gavuzzi pushed too hard during the preceding three days when he had managed to regain the lead from Payne? Or had Payne pushed too hard this day in front of his local fans?

No one greeted Ray and me as we ran into Claremore this morning 70 years later. In the same manner I entered, I quietly left Claremore and quietly entered Foyil, chatting a few minutes with the locals about their hero. However, in my mind, it was not quietly. I could see the crowds and hear their loud greetings that had greeted Andy Payne.

After leaving Foyil, someone whom I had only met through e-mail, Steve Harrison, joined me for a few miles of running together. He later e-mailed to express his enjoyment of our meeting and running together. He also wrote, "What a great and awesome God we serve! It is my prayer, and that of my family, that the remaining days of your run will bring glory to our Father's name, that you continue to be blessed and free from injury, and that the Father would protect you, Marcy, your children, and, of course, your parents as they are with you."

Steve would e-mail me several times during my run, offering encouragement and praise to God. Making new friends is one of life's rich blessings, isn't it?

Later in the day, I ran into Chelsea where I stopped in to meet the county commissioner. Why would I take the time and make the effort to do that? Well, he had a familiar name. His name was Jerry Payne, and he is the nephew of Andy Payne. It was a pleasure to meet him and spend a few minutes hearing more Andy Payne stories.

When I reached Chelsea on old Route 66, I couldn't resist running a half-mile detour through the old downtown. I have a book that has a picture of Andy Payne finishing first in that day's 50-mile segment in downtown Chelsea after his incredible run. The picture shows Payne finishing through a narrow corridor of hordes of people crowded together in the middle of main street to see their local hero finish first in that day's run.

Many of the buildings in downtown Chelsea look exactly as they did in that 1928 photo. It was a thrill to run through town and replay that Bunion Derby day. The locals had to be whispering as I ran down the middle of that same street, smiling broadly and acknowledging with waves of my hand the imagined, cheering crowd. Instead of running through a corridor of people, I ran through a corridor of cars parked on the side of Main Street.

After finishing the day's run about seven miles past Chelsea, Marcy and I headed the 60 miles back home for my last night at home — hopefully, the last night at home for five weeks. During the day, Marcy had said, "Well, we aren't going to get in as many miles today, but I sure have enjoyed meeting a bunch of really nice people." I could only add "amen" to that.

Day 48, May 14.
Chelsea, OK to Miami, OK — 40.7 miles.
"Follow the Narrow Brick Road"

NOT ONE TO pass up an opportunity to help someone, good friend Kevin King volunteered to be my crew for the day, his birthday, giving Marcy a break. It was a little more difficult to leave the house this morning, knowing it would likely (hopefully) be another five weeks before I would be back home. Though it was a one-hour drive back to where I had stopped the previous day, I was back running at about 7 a.m. Today's run took me through Vinita, White Oak, Afton, and Narcissa before finishing in Miami — Miami, Oklahoma, that is.

Just past Afton was a three-mile section of the most interesting Route 66 pavement I had seen. The pavement was only nine feet wide, about the size of one lane on today's roads. It looked more like a running/bike path than a road. On both edges of the pavement was a three-inch curb. Just off to each side of the narrow road was gravel. I assume the gravel was in case two cars passed each other; each car could have two tires on the pavement and two tires on gravel. I'm not sure how it would work; not only did two cars not pass, not even one car went by me in those three miles.

Just before I reached Miami in the afternoon, an Oklahoma highway patrolman stopped as I was taking a break alongside Kevin's van. He asked, "Didn't I see you running in Vinita this morning?" That had been about 30 miles earlier, and he seemed a little puzzled. I explained my run, and he wished me luck. However, I've always had a suspicion that he might have told his kids that night, "I thought I had heard it all. You won't believe the line a guy gave me today."

At the end of today's run, Dad, Mom, and daughter Heather rejoined me with the motor home. Heather had just finished her first year at the University of Arkansas and was now going to experience a week on the road. Now that the motor home was back with me, it seemed official: we're on the road again! We enjoyed being hosted by cousin Linda and her husband George Childers at their home in Miami. They showed us around town and treated us to a pizza feast at a local restaurant.

On my website I received an e-mail from someone who had a very good understanding of what my crew and I were experiencing. Audra Bell wrote, "I am the daughter of Raymond Bell who ran across the United States in the Trans-America race of 1993 and 1995. I had the pleasure of being one of his crew members in the 1995 trek, and it was one of the most exciting experiences of my life." During each of the three years in 1993 through 1995, there had been organized stage races across the United States (similar to the Bunion Derby). Raymond Bell had been one of the top runners in two of these races, in which an average of ten runners finished each year.

I also received an e-mail from Bonnie Busch, an outstanding ultra-marathon runner whom I had met at a race in Iowa several years earlier. Like Audra, Bonnie had also helped runners in the Trans-America races. She wrote, "My heart is with you. Many of my summers were spent watching, dreaming, and joining the Trans Am runs of 1993-1995."

Additionally, an e-mail was received this day from someone who had also been a part of inspiring me to run across the country. During the 95 days of February 21 to May 26, 1990, Bill Schultz had run solo across the United States. He did not have a permanent crew, but depended on help from running friends across the United States. He e-mailed from where he lives near Philadelphia to say that he had run many of the same roads that I had up to this day. He added, "I'm sure you are having a great adventure ... I did." He, like few others, knew exactly how great the adventure really was.

Bill later wrote again and said, "Can't tell you how much fun I've had the past few minutes looking back over my log ... with you running basically the same route." His next e-mail message included this comment after he had looked at my pictures on the website, "I must admit, it's going to be hard not to get involved all over again." At the time, I wasn't sure what he meant. Now, as I write this nearly seven years later, I think I have a better understanding of what Bill meant.

On one hand, it is very enjoyable to think back through the journey and relive it the best you can. On the other hand, it is emotional in that you know you can never truly fully capture or relive the thrill. Every effort to recapture the excitement seems like a cheap imitation that never comes close to approaching the original. As much as I would like to live it again, deep inside, I know it's an experience that cannot be duplicated here on earth. Sometimes, it's easier to just not go there. For the past several years, I have often elected "to just not go there" in order to enjoy the present blessings in life and not live in the past. The decision "to go there" and write this book has been joyful, yet challenging, at times.

My run for this day had gone just as planned with no surprises. However, it was not so in the Bunion Derby. In a surprising turnaround from the preceding day, Gavuzzi beat Payne in the Chelsea to Miami segment by 1 hour and 40 minutes to reduce Payne's lead to 13 minutes. Maybe Payne had indeed pushed too hard for his hometown fans the preceding day.

Day 49, May 15.
Miami, OK to Joplin, MO — 36.7 miles.
"Run Out of Town"

ANDY PAYNE NEVER had it this good! Arranged by George, I had a police escort through Miami, through Commerce and all the way to Quapaw — the first 12 miles of the run this morning. The police car with its flashing lights followed me that entire way. Drivers and pedestrians alike had to wonder why I was being run out of town by the police. It must have looked like a modern-day scene from an old western movie: the bad guy gets chased out of town by the local sheriff and his posse.

I did not mix in any walking, and ran faster than normal, during those 12 miles for fear of being run over by the police car. In downtown Commerce, the locals even had the lights flashing on all the emergency vehicles and the traffic blocked as I turned onto Mickey Mantle Boulevard. I wrote down the names of my escorts so I would not forget the kindness and excitement they provided that morning. Thank you, Danny Green and Glenn Johnston of the Miami Police Department and Roger Nagl and Chief Bob Baine of the Commerce Police Department.

When I reached Quapaw, running friend Jodie D'Avignon (Mr. D, as the students called him — and with good reason) had several of his high school biology and chemistry students on the street in front of the school to greet me. Jodie had run a few miles with me in the morning before going to school. We met some really nice people in Quapaw, including Terri Truelove who joined me for a couple of miles of running. Emilee, daughter of Terri and her husband Jerry, would later e-mail encouragement from Washington D.C. where she worked as a media consultant.

One of Mr. D's students whom I had met (Matt Robertson) later e-mailed and said, "Just wishin' you luck, so good luck and swim a little for me in south carolina-alright!" I thought, "If

I get to South Carolina, I will be swimming for hundreds and hundreds of people who have been a part of my journey through encouragement and prayers."

A few miles on down Route 66, I left my home state and ran the 13 miles across the southeast corner of Kansas. In Baxter Springs, Kansas, I met fireman Art Mallory and newspaperman John Hacker. People like Art and John were always very encouraging, and I always left feeling energized for the task ahead.

A little later in the day while leaving Galena, Kansas, I was startled when a policeman drove by and on his loudspeaker said, "Good luck, man." I wondered how he knew what I was doing. I later found out that he had stopped by the motor home on the side of the road to see if Dad and Mom were having problems. They had filled him in on our adventure.

I finished the day's run at the intersection of Highways 66 and 71 in Joplin, Missouri, having run in three states during the day. We had visitors for dinner at the KOA Campground where we stayed for the night. Pastor Roy and his wife, Norma Emmons, along with their granddaughters Stephanie and Audra, joined us before they headed home after visiting the Precious Moments art gallery in nearby Carthage.

The Bunion Derby runners had also done this same Miami to Joplin stretch in one day, their 47th day versus my 49th day. The day I had taken off, as well as the following short day, had dropped me two days behind the Bunion Derby race. On the Miami, Oklahoma to Joplin, Missouri segment, Payne had reversed the previous day's results and bettered Gavuzzi by nearly 90 minutes. Payne's overall lead was now 1 hour, 43 minutes.

It had been a thrill for me to run the same roads while dreaming of the Bunion Derby 70 years prior. I had run in their footsteps from Los Angeles, California to Joplin, Missouri. After previously reading books and newspaper accounts and looking at pictures of the race, I often could visualize what it must have been like to be a part of the Bunion Derby as I ran down Route 66.

It had been wonderful *Running With Payne* and dreaming of the race; however, the next day I was going to say goodbye forever to the Bunion Derby. While the race continued on Route 66 to Chicago, I was going to head south toward Arkansas. In planning the run, I had nixed the thought of going through Chicago and on to New York City similar to the Bunion Derby. Getting out of the Los Angeles area was challenge enough; I didn't want to negotiate through any more huge cities. Therefore, I had planned to run Route 66 to Joplin and then stay south.

Then I had the strange thought that I would like to run through the University of Arkansas campus at Fayetteville, Arkansas, where, as I mentioned earlier, daughter Heather had just finished her freshman year. Why I would want to do this I don't really know other than I knew I would always have those special memories any time I went there to visit her. Sure enough, I have gone there several times since that day, and it always rekindled the pleasant memories of a special day. But I'm ahead of myself, that day is still three days away.

Although I'm not running alongside the Bunion Derby day after day, don't stop reading; updates and the concluding summary of the Bunion Derby will come a little later.

9

SO LONG, ROUTE 66

Day 50, May 16.

Joplin, MO to Jane, MO — 43.0 miles.

"Goodness Snakes Alive"

THIS WAS ANOTHER beautiful day in the Ozarks, with no clouds and little wind. I resumed the journey in Joplin, but instead of following Route 66 northeast, I went south out of Joplin on Highway 71 and would go almost straight south for three days. Going south for three days doesn't make much sense considering that the goal is to go from west to east across the country.

Today's run took me through the Missouri towns of Neosho, Goodman, Anderson, Pineville, and ending two miles from Jane. One of the most startling and puzzling things that happened on the cross-country run occurred just a few miles past Neosho. I was running on the shoulder of the busy highway with my visor pulled down low on my forehead and my eyes gazing down at the pavement. I could only see about four feet in front of me and was lost in my thoughts.

Suddenly, I heard something hitting and then sliding on the pavement in front of me. Instinctively, I jumped straight up just in time to feel the wind and see something slide under my airborne feet. When I landed after my vertical jump of eight inches (two inches more than normal), I turned in time to see a four-foot-long black snake sliding to a halt on the edge of the highway shoulder 12 feet behind me.

I cautiously walked back for a closer look. It had a stunned, "what happened?" look on its face. Well, actually, we both had stunned, "what happened?" looks on our faces. Whether the snake was thrown from or fell off a vehicle, I never knew. There had been some hay-hauling trucks that had gone by earlier. I would prefer to believe the snake fell off a truck.

Whatever may have happened, I was thankful for God's protection on the run. Had the snake hit me instead of sliding under, I'm not sure my heart would have taken it. You can be assured that I ran with my head up the rest of the day.

A sign had me chuckling to myself as I ran between Joplin and Neosho earlier in the day. I noticed a large metal building with a big sign saying "Biker's Boutique." On the front of the building, several items were listed, including leather jackets, saddlebags, helmets, chaps, and chrome. It was the last thing on the list that seemed out of place: lingerie. I guess that's the "boutique" part of the business name. Though I had some questions about this, I didn't stop at the store, nor did I ask any bikers. Some bikers may take exception to being asked about their lingerie shopping.

The old motor home had worked like a charm so far. We encountered the first major problem today as a large hole had been knocked in the fiberglass disposal tank. Afterward, Dad had driven several miles to Bentonville to buy fiberglass coating. He worked several hours in the RV park this evening trying to fix the hole. It had been a frustrating day for Dad, but I had taken advantage of the beautiful day to cover 43 miles, the longest mileage day of the run so far.

Day 51, May 17.
Jane, MO to Fayetteville, AR — 36.0 miles.
"Toed You So"

HEADING STRAIGHT SOUTH on Highway 71, I crossed the state line into Arkansas. The hills, rocky bluffs, streams, thick forests, and numerous golf courses made for a beautiful run in the morning. After entering Arkansas, I ran through the towns of Bella Vista, Bentonville, Rogers, and Springdale.

Going through Bentonville, I kept watch for its two most renowned resident families: the Waltons of Wal-Mart fame and the Tysons of Tyson Chicken fame. They must not have gotten word that I was running through town; they didn't come out to meet me either on the road or at Bethel Baptist Church where we attended the Sunday morning worship service.

I finished the day's run about four miles north of Fayetteville. With just a few miles to go to complete the run, long-time friends Randy and Lynna Blackwell of nearby Siloam Springs found us taking a break alongside the road. Randy and Dad drove the motor home on to Fayetteville and found a cozy campground. Lynna and Mom crewed the last few miles from the Blackwells' car.

After we all arrived at the campground, Arkansas student Jennifer Carter, Heather's good friend from our hometown, also joined us for a feast on Subway sandwiches. The highlight (?) of the evening was everyone sitting around and commenting how ugly my toes were. The toes had been through a lot in the last 51 days and definitely showed some wear and tear. In reality, my toes were not very good-looking even before I started the run. Toes are one of the lesser attributes of most long-distance runners. Of course, many think that mental capacity must be one of the lesser attributes of most long-distance runners.

It was not unusual to receive some laughs when I checked the website at the end of the day's run. My brother Craig livened our evening when he sent this one: "A little boy was walking out of church Sunday morning, and as he shook the pastor's hand he said, 'When I grow up I am going to give you a lot of money.' The pastor, somewhat puzzled said, 'Why are you going to do that, Tommy?' To which Tommy replied, 'Because my dad says you are the poorest pastor we have ever had.' "

Day 52, May 18.
Fayetteville, AR to Mountainburg, AR — 41.0 miles.
"On Track"

AFTER GETTING OFF to an early morning start, I enjoyed one of the highlights of my journey: running around the University of Arkansas campus with Heather. Dad, Heather, and I also ran a commemorative mile on the manicured university track. The University of Arkansas is well known for its outstanding achievements and numerous national championships in cross-country and track. What in the world was I doing? I was not only not making any eastward progress for three days, but I was also now running in circles around a track.

All too soon, we were taking pictures at the large university entrance sign and then resuming the southward trek on Highway 71. The state was in the process of building a new super highway through the hilly country between Fayetteville and Fort Smith. It was not quite completed, so I had to run on the old, dangerous two-lane highway, which had little or no shoulder. Entering the Boston Mountains area, a sign stated: "7 People Killed in 3 Years, Don't be the Next One." That caught my attention! My goal was to get through this stretch and not be that next one.

The climbs through this mountainous area were challenging and the weather was hot, but the hazy views of distant rolling hills and Fort Smith Lake in the valley were spectacular. I often noticed the contrasting scents of pine trees and burning brakes from descending vehicles. (Or was the burning smell from the soles of my shoes?) After finishing 41 miles, we drove about five miles further down the mountain to camp at Fort Smith Lake. Dad, Mom, and Heather enjoyed hiking and exploring the lake and the park. I enjoyed doing nothing. My 41 miles of hiking and exploring, mostly in the Boston Mountains, had been more than enough on a warm, tiring day. Though it was a very warm day, we experienced a snowstorm in the motor home that evening. As Mom was getting an opened, but full, box of cornstarch out of a high cabinet, it fell off the shelf, bounced off a few things, including Mom, before finally hitting the floor. Cornstarch flew in every direction and, instantaneously, much of the motor home turned into a white winterland. Just like in real life, sometimes it's better to just find the humor of the moment and keep on going. It's best not to let those things take the "starch" out of the enjoyable things in life.

Day 53, May 19.
Mountainburg, AR to Ozark, AR — 42.7 miles.
"Adversarial Relationship"

THIS WAS ANOTHER day of big hills with beautiful views, accompanied with much heat and humidity. I finished the southward leg on Highway 71 by going through the towns of Mountainburg (what does that tell you about the terrain?), Dean's Market (didn't see him), and into Alma. At last, I turned back east on Highway 64 and ran through Dyer, Mulberry, and into Ozark. Yes, I was again heading in an easterly direction, which, when you think of it, is critical if one wants to reach the Atlantic Ocean.

When I reached Alma in the morning, I saw an old adversary that I hadn't seen in over 400 miles — not since Yukon, Oklahoma. This adversary and I certainly had our differences during the previous several weeks. I had called him several names over the previous seven weeks. Come to think of it, he didn't have much regard for me either. Just the sight of him brought back memories of large trucks, high winds, snow, and fence crossings during our times together in California, Arizona, New Mexico, Texas, and Oklahoma. I didn't care much to be around him, and I can only assume he felt the same way about me.

Who was this adversary? It was none other than the dreaded Interstate 40, of course. As I crossed over I-40 on the overpass, there was some tension and coolness in the air as we gave each other the wary eye. Although we would see each other only via overpasses as I ran on Highway 64 the next three days, we were already thinking about our next confrontation. That confrontation would take place one week later on the Mississippi River Bridge, at which time I would have to run on I-40 in order to go into Memphis, Tennessee.

He and I both knew that the Mississippi River Bridge was not big enough for the both of us. He had thrown some difficult things my way, but I was confident that he would not stop my journey. However, I would find out later that he had a surprise up his sleeve for our next confrontation. That last showdown in Memphis would be one that we would never forget (or forgive).

At the end of the day, we camped at beautiful Ozark Park on the banks of the Arkansas River. We met some very nice people, including the park manager who was from Perkins, Oklahoma, not far from our hometown.

Day 54, May 20.
Ozark, AR to London, AR — 43.7 miles.
"Feather Buster"

ARKANSAS SEEMS TO have small towns located about six miles or so apart. Today's run went through the "major metropolitan" areas of Altus, Coal Hill, Hartman, Clarksville, Lamar, Piney, and finished at London. Running along the shores of Lake Dardanelle made for a beautiful end to a long day on the road.

Early in the day, our hometown friends, Eric and Laurie Freeman and their children, found us on Highway 64 and had lunch with us. They were heading to Little Rock to visit relatives. You may remember Eric from his two days of road-crewing in western Oklahoma. Given all the long hours on the road and seeing only strangers, it was always very encouraging to see friends. The Freemans would also join us the next night for dinner.

Since my mom's family had its roots in London, Arkansas, she had looked forward to getting there and finding some of her relatives. Marcy, son Justin, and daughter Nicole drove three hours from home to join the rest of us for the evening. Heather would go back with Marcy the following day so she could start her summer job as a counselor at a Christian youth camp. Having been with us for six days, she probably had enough of the motor home confinement. Justin would take her place for a few days of road duty.

In Arkansas, I often noticed chicken feathers scattered along the shoulders of the road. I gave that some thought this day and think I figured out why. As chickens are being transported to market in large trucks, undoubtedly there are some smart ones who operate in a similar fashion to a military person or a good outdoorsman. The smart chickens leave trails of feathers in hopes of either being rescued or escaping and finding their way back home.

It's amazing the thoughts that enter a sun-baked, energy-deprived brain. In light of that, I know what you are thinking. You're thinking that comment about "being out in the sun too long" from the greeter at the church in Grants, New Mexico really did bother me. Certainly not! I had forgotten it until you just now thought of it and brought it up.

Day 55, May 21.
London, AR to Plumerville, AR — 39.6 miles.
"Signs, Signs, Everywhere Signs"

WELL, I DIDN'T get my donuts! Early in the morning, Marcy drove me from the campground back to London, where I would resume running from yesterday's stopping point. She then drove along my intended route into the town of Russellville to buy donuts for breakfast for everyone back at camp. Somehow, we missed each other on her return trip and I didn't get those donuts for which I had a craving. I later consoled myself with a convenience store stop, eating three very large chocolate donuts and drinking a bottle of Gatorade.

I ran by an old building that had a sign that read "Not responsible for acidents." The missing "c" from the word accidents seemed to be contradictory to the sign. Someone was responsible for at least that one accident. I also ran by a real estate sign that read "Pardade of Homes." I never figured out what a "pardade" was.

As the temperature had risen later in the day, I went into a Pottsville convenience store to buy some liquids. I always wondered what people were thinking when I came in attired in a sweaty shirt and running shorts.

As the middle-aged lady looked up from behind the counter, I asked, "Is this the way to the Atlantic Ocean?" I let her stammer for a moment before I explained what I was doing. She was cordial and wished me well as I departed. However, I'm not so sure she believed me. After I left, I could imagine her calling her husband and saying, "You're not going to believe what just happened."

Running along during the day, I met three ladies out for a 40-mile bike ride in the afternoon heat. I enjoyed spending a few minutes and sharing my adventure with Mae Rene Rose of Russellville, Donna Moore of Clinton, and Maxine Higgins of Little Rock.

As I ran by a house later in the day, an elderly lady, checking her mailbox, asked me, "Getting exercise?"

I replied, "You might say that. I'm running from the west coast to the east coast.

She then proceeded to sum up the whole adventure in one short sentence: "Well, if you keep going, you'll get there."

I thought, "How true, but it is only true if you keep going in the right direction and not straight south like I did for three days."

I continued my small-town running, passing through Russellville, Pottsville, Atkins, Kenwood, Morrilton, and finished in Plumerville. After the run, we drove into Conway and camped at Toad Suck Lock and Dam Park. Really, that's the name! Seriously, look it up on a map.

Wouldn't you like to meet the committee who came up with that name? What were they thinking? In our politically correct world of protest, I anticipated seeing little frogs carrying signs and marching at the entrance of the park, protesting against the name of the park. Could you blame them?

We did have a wonderful time in the park that evening. We were joined by good friends Eric and Carrie Platner from Little Rock and the Freemans. After dinner, we enjoyed a watermelon and had a wonderful time of fellowship together. (I didn't need to add "together," did I? It's difficult to have fellowship not together.)

How about a Bunion Derby update? We last left the Bunion Derby in Joplin, Missouri, as it headed toward Chicago on Route 66. Andy Payne had a 1 hour, 40 minute lead over Englishman Peter Gavuzzi after 47 days of racing.

Gavuzzi began pushing the pace during days 48 through 55, as the racers continued running on Route 66 through Springfield toward St. Louis. On day 48, Gavuzzi finished one hour and five minutes ahead of Payne. On days 49 through 52, Payne managed to stay with Gavuzzi, and they generally finished together. However, on day 53, Gavuzzi finished over one hour ahead of Payne and regained the overall lead.

On day 54, Gavuzzi ran the 45.6-mile segment in an incredible 6 hours and 11 minutes, finishing over an hour ahead of Payne. By the time they reached East St. Louis after 55 days, Gavuzzi had a 1 hour and 50 minute lead over Payne.

Day 56, May 22.
Plumerville, AR to El Paso, AR — 37.9 miles.
"Drag Trafficking"

EMBARKING ON THIS journey eight weeks ago this morning, I never thought it would go this well and this quickly. I would hit the 2,000-mile mark on this afternoon. That sounds like a long way, and I felt and ran as though it had been that long.

Though it was not as hot and humid as it had been in previous days, my legs were tired right from the start of the day. I had averaged 41 miles per day the previous six warm days, and it had taken a toll — I was dragging. It was a struggling day as I endured heavy Memorial-weekend traffic, narrow shoulders on the road, and a couple of obscene gestures.

After running through Menifee, Conway, Hamlet, and Vilonia, I called it a day at the 2,000-mile mark near El Paso. It was a relief to finally reach our campsite at scenic El Paso City Park. You know it was a difficult day when I don't write much about it.

It must have been a real tiring day. Mom's journal said that at the end of the day I talked about how much longer it was going to take to finish. I decided that the best finishing day would be on a Saturday. I could push the miles and finish in three more weeks, or take it a little easier and finish in four weeks. Which one do you think I would choose?

Day 57, May 23.
El Paso, AR to Bald Knob, AR — 41.5 miles.
"Dog Gone Running"

IT WAS A "grande" morning as I left the hacienda in El Paso. I was off to an early 5:58 a.m. start as I was "gunning" to get to Beebe by 8:30. At Beebe I headed northeast on Highway 367 and ran through McRae, Garner, Searcy, and Judsonia, before finishing in Bald Knob.

I'm glad to report there were no "hair-raising" incidents on my run to Bald Knob. A cloudy day kept the temperature down, and I felt a little more rested today.

Over the preceding weeks, it had been a joy to run with several people, both renewing friendships and making new ones. However, on this day I ran with the most exuberant runner yet.

On a two-lane road a few miles before Searcy, I was startled by something running up the ditch from behind me. I turned to see a very pretty female bird dog. She was so excited, it seemed as though she had just been set free. I instantly liked the dog and soon figured out why. She tirelessly ran through fields, fences, gardens, streams, and mud holes as she observed and explored everything around her. It dawned on me that this dog epitomized how I had felt during most of my journey, running across open country eagerly taking in all the sights, sounds, and smells. I also realized that all the miles, coupled with the aches and pains and traffic, had in recent days somewhat dulled the excitement that I had earlier experienced. However, witnessing this dog's exuberance rekindled some of the thrill and excitement that I had felt earlier in the journey.

One big difference between the dog and me was the dog's lack of road experience. I had to agonizingly watch her blindly dart across the highway several times, narrowly escaping getting hit by speeding vehicles. It was also not fun having to endure the scorn of braking drivers, wondering why I had brought my dog out on the road. They were thinking, "It's stupid enough for a human to be running down these narrow roads, but to have his untrained dog darting across the roads — he's a real moron." Maybe they were right on that last part, but it wasn't because of the dog.

Undoubtedly for the good, on my next break at the motor home, my friend wandered away — not to be seen again. We had run together for 40 minutes, during which she probably ran eight zig-zagging miles to my four straight miles. Yet, I had enjoyed the company and appreciated her love of running and exploring.

Dad had a frustrating afternoon. One week after the first hole, another hole was knocked in the fiberglass holding tank, which meant we could not use the motor home sink and bathroom. That was the perfect excuse to get a hotel room for the night. During the day, Dad, Mom, and Justin had driven into Searcy to buy some more fiberglass patching material. Dad and Justin worked several hours patching it up that evening. Looking at the positive side, the shower, beds, and TV in the hotel were a really nice change from the confines of the motor home.

Day 58, May 24.
Bald Knob, AR to Wynne, AR — 41.0 miles.
"You Can Bank on It"

MIGRATING EASTWARD ON Highway 64, I passed through some interesting small towns. I managed to escape Worden with no trouble. I mastered Augusta, and came up five miles short in my attempt for Wynne. To top it off, I started in Bald Knob. If you're not shaking your head at this moment, you need to read this paragraph again — slowly.

What a difference a day can make in the terrain! After many hills the past few days, today's run was through nothing but flat farmland. The only hill was a very long, narrow bridge over the White River.

It was obvious to me today that few, if any, road engineers are runners. The slope to the shoulders on Highway 64 seemed similar to the banking on the curves at the Daytona Speedway. It would almost take a contortionist to run comfortably on those shoulders. Running against the traffic, the feet and ankles angled away from the road, while the rest of the body compensated by leaning back toward the road. It felt as though the bottom of the left running shoe had rolled up on the inside part of my ankle, and the bottom of the right shoe had rolled up on the outside part of my ankle. Additionally, the five toes on each foot were crammed against one side of the shoe in about half the normal space.

It made for a tough day on the feet and knees. I wondered if there would be any lasting effects similar to the very windy day near Flagstaff that had altered my running style, resulting in injury.

Day 59, May 25.
Wynne, AR to Marion, AR — 41.5 miles.
"Passing Grade"

A MEMORIAL DAY Monday! At the end of the day, I deserved a shirt that stated "I survived Memorial Day weekend on Arkansas highways!" Football and basketball commentators talk about ill-advised passes. They should have seen the numerous risky passes by vehicles on the two-lane road I ran on all day. There were several close calls, but thankfully no accidents, at least that I saw. I have never seen so many RVs, campers, boats, water devices, and fishing poles — all heading home, I assume, after the long weekend.

Today's run was a continuance run through wheat and rice fields and included the small towns of Wynne, Levesque, Parkin,

Earle, Crawfordsville, Ebony, and ending in Marion. The small shoulders seemed to have less slope on them today — or maybe I just had gotten used to running at an angle.

Since Marion is only 11 miles from the Mississippi River, tomorrow's run will take me through Memphis, Tennessee. I had dreaded that part — and with good reason, as it would turn out! An Arkansas patrolman told us that the north bridge (the I-40 bridge) had a pedestrian walkway and was the one we would want to run across. We were glad about that and made plans on getting through Memphis tomorrow. All our planning would go to waste!

On the long roads near Fayetteville, Arkansas.

10

I-40 SHOWDOWN

Day 60, May 26.
Marion, AR to Oakland, TN — 45.0 miles.
"Singing the Memphis Blues"

YET ANOTHER CHALLENGE — this would prove to be one of the most memorable, if not infamous, days of the whole journey. This was the day I had to face my foe from previous weeks: the dreaded Interstate 40.

After leaving Marion early in the morning, I soon reached I-40. I delayed our meeting for a ways as I ran on an adjacent service road. However, the service road soon ended, and I then had to climb up an embankment and start running on the menacing highway.

I had just gotten up on I-40 and was running over a small bridge when I accidentally stepped on a circular piece of wire. The wire flipped up and caught the other foot in mid-stride. The next thing I knew, I was sprawled out on the bridge. I quickly scrambled back onto my feet, wondering how many motorists had just witnessed my ungraceful fall. I spent the next few minutes picking gravel out of my palms. What a way to start the morning! I-40 had gotten in the first lick. It wasn't going to get better any time soon.

I soon was excited to see the big old bridge, the Mississippi River Bridge. I was finished with Arkansas! However, when I reached the long, long, long bridge, I realized that, contrary to what three different people (including the Arkansas patrolman) had told us, the bridge did not have a pedestrian lane. As I had originally thought, it was the Highway 55 bridge down the river to the south that had the separate pedestrian walkway. I-40 had gotten in the second lick.

On the bridge, there was about two feet between the white line and the side of the bridge. Peering over the side of the bridge, I realized that it was a long, long way down to the water. I cautiously ran across the bridge, hoping the three lanes of morning rush hour traffic would not crowd the white line. There was no place to go if they did. I quickened my pace and was very relieved to finally reach the other side safely. However, it wasn't going to get better any time soon.

Shortly after crossing the Mississippi, high winds and a heavy downpour hit the Memphis area, all during morning rush hour traffic. Of course, I had no rain gear and my crew was somewhere else, having their own problems negotiating Memphis traffic. With the darkness and the heavy rain, I felt extremely vulnerable as I ran along the shoulder against heavy traffic on I-40. I felt very desperate as I ran by the Danny Thomas Hospital (hoping I didn't end up in there), looking for my turn that would get me off the stinking I-40, which had gotten in the third lick. It wasn't going to get better any time soon.

Per my planned route, I needed to turn east on Highway 1 shortly after the Mississippi River Bridge. After running for several miles in the downpour, I knew that I somehow had missed the turn somewhere along the way. (I found out later that the Highway 1 exit off I-40 was not marked.)

Stopping under an overpass to get out of the rain, I pulled

out the plastic bag containing the piece of paper on which I had written directions. The bag had leaked, and the soaked directions were hardly legible. Now what? I was lost and I had no idea where the motor home, my sanctuary, was. It wasn't going to get better any time soon.

I decided to get off I-40 and try to find my way to Highway 1, the planned route. I used a crosswalk overpass to get up and over I-40 and into a neighborhood. As it turned out, this would not be the neighborhood I would have chosen to run through. It was a rough-looking area. It was probably fortunate for me that it was still raining very hard and no one was on the streets — no one except a lost, drenched, and drowning runner.

Needing directions, I saw an elderly man sitting in a wheelchair on a screened-in front porch. As I approached, I saw that he was also hooked up to a bottle of oxygen. I thought, "That's all this poor man needs is for some weird, fruitcake stranger coming to his door in a rainstorm. I gave him a most cheerful, "Good morning, sir. I'm lost and I'm looking for Highway 1. Could you point me in the right direction?"

That's precisely what he did; and all that he did. He just pointed behind him. I thanked him and sloshed off down the street. It now had been two hours of constant hard rain, and the streets were becoming flooded. And I still didn't know where I was, much less where my crew was. It wasn't going to get better any time soon.

Let me just say it plainly: the street signs in Memphis were the worst of any place I ran. Let me just say it plainly: Memphis was the worst place of any place I ran. I still have nightmares when I think of Memphis.

I eventually found Highway 1. As miserable as the soaked, flooded, drowning running conditions were, it was actually God's blessing that it was so. I ran through some very tough and dangerous areas. Due to the heavy rain, there was minimal traffic and no one walking the streets.

I remembered that on the east side of Memphis I needed to be on Highway 64. As I sloshed through Memphis, I had to stop a few times and ask directions. At a real estate agency's office, I knocked on the door, opened it slightly and poked my head through the doorway. They said "Come on in." I opened the door wider so they could see a tall, skinny guy in drenched, dripping running clothes and a cap visor drooping from all the rain. I think they then appreciated me telling them that it would be better if I just stood right there and asked for directions. They told me how to find Highway 64.

It had been about 7 hours and 30 miles since I had seen my crew early in the morning. You can't imagine our collective relief when I got to Highway 64 on the east side of Memphis and found the motor home and crew waiting in a parking lot. As Mom wrote, "This was one of the hardest days of the whole run."

I ran a few more miles in the afternoon and finished my longest day of 45 miles in Oakland, Tennessee. Marcy had driven out to join the motor home for the rest of the run, while Mom, along with Justin, would return to Oklahoma to keep things running on the home front.

Day 61, May 27.
Oakland, TN to Bolivar, TN — 35.0 miles.
"No Shoulder To Cry On"

AFTER A LONG and tough previous day through Memphis, coupled with a restless night, it was predictably a difficult day. After all the rain the previous day, the humidity and heat were quite noticeable. Additionally, I had left the flat farmland behind and was now getting back into hills.

I should never have complained about the severe slope on the shoulders of the road in Arkansas — at least it had a shoulder. After resuming in Oakland in the morning, I ran into

Sommerville on a nice, wide, flat shoulder. Shortly after Sommerville, I came around a corner to face a two-lane highway without any shoulder. The white line on the edge of the pavement was right against a growth of tall weeds.

There's always the question of how bold (or ignorant?) you want to be with the drivers. Do you hold your position on the edge of the road and trust the drivers will give you some space? What if two cars are meeting at your location and they don't have room to give? I'm neither a very bold nor trusting runner; I tend to step off the pavement and give the cars the space. I always assume that I will come out the worse if a car and I try to occupy the same space at the same time.

The weeds next to the edge of the road made for miserable running conditions. I tried running on an adjacent road bed that had been laid in preparation for an additional two lanes. However, I would continually bog down in the mud left from yesterday's monsoon. It was a day of stepping on the road, off the road, on the road, off the road, etc.

I ran by two mental health institutions in the Bolivar area. Contrary to the suggestions I had received over the past few weeks, I did not stop in for an evaluation. However, after the past three days, I did entertain the thought for a bit. (Friend Dennis Queen wrote, "It's possible that you could be accused of running away from the asylum.") Though I didn't stop, I did run on the grass along the front of one of the mental institutions. Immediately afterward, I noticed that my legs felt better about themselves.

At the end of this difficult day, I did use good wisdom by disappointedly calling it a day after only 35 miles. We had an enjoyable conversation with a nice park ranger at Chickasaw State Park where we camped for the night. Most park rangers seemed to catch the thrill of a cross-country run. The frustrating day didn't end on the roads; Dad spent another three hours patching the holding tank again. We may get there in pieces, but both the motor home and I were going to get to the Atlantic.

Mike Fanning, who had been a big help in the first two days of the run, sent this good thought, "From reading your journal, I've learned that wide shoulders are important to runners. Wide shoulders are also very important for Christians to find strength to go on. God always has wide shoulders, doesn't He? What a blessing to know God, the God who has infinitely wide shoulders."

Day 62, May 28.
Bolivar, TN to Corinth, MS — 45.0 miles.
"Change, Of Course"

HIGHWAY 64, ADIOS and good riddance! With those, and other choice words, I walked off Highway 64, climbed some steep rocks between the bridges of a divided highway, slipped through some shrubbery, climbed over a guardrail, and headed south on Highway 45. This highway had a wide shoulder. I was free at last, free to run without continually stepping off the road into the weeds.

After the many difficult miles with no shoulder on Highway 64, we had enacted a new plan on the fly. At Selmar, Tennessee, I decided to abandon H-64 and head south on Highway 45 to Corinth, Mississippi. At Corinth, I would again turn east on Highway 72. I was hoping and praying that these roads had shoulders. I certainly had not planned on running through Mississippi, but miserable running conditions had made me desperate to try a different route.

Not only were the running conditions miserable, the weather was also getting that way. It was 91 degrees when I ran through Selmar. Oh yes, I remembered those cooler-than-expected temperatures out west.

As I sat in the motor home at the end of the day, I was amazed to realize that I now had been on the road for two months. I was also amazed that I was fortunate enough (or dumb enough) to have completed 45 miles on two of the last three days.

Then again, my 45 miles on two of the last three days were nothing compared to Tom Andrews' two days. I received an e-mail this day from Tom, whom I had not met, saying, "Way to go, Randy. I am a follower of Jesus Christ and just returned from France where I ran 48 hours straight in the Surgeres 48-hour race. Set the American record for 40-44 age group at 205 miles. I admire what you are doing and send my energy to you. 'Those who wait (hope) on the Lord will renew their strength; ... they will run and not grow weary, walk and not grow faint.' Take care, wish I was with you, buddy!"

When I started at Santa Monica Beach, it had been impossible to imagine that two months later I would be 2,249 miles down the road and sitting in Mississippi. Of course, one reason why it had been impossible to imagine this was that I had never planned to run through Mississippi in the first place. What was I doing in Mississippi? Whatever it was, I wouldn't be there long.

Day 63, May 29.
Corinth, MS to Barton, AL — 39.5 miles.
"Narrow Minded"

AFTER A FEW miles of running this morning, I soon had reservations concerning my decision to leave Highway 64 in Tennessee due to it not having shoulders. As I headed east on Highway 72 out of Corinth, Mississippi, I discovered that this highway had 15-inch shoulders.

Granted, 15 inches is better than having no shoulder and the white line on the edge of the road against weeds. However, 15 inches seemed really narrow when cars and trucks whizzed by within a couple of feet. At 6 feet, 4 inches, and 175 pounds, I was slightly thin, but I didn't fit within 15 inches very well.

I nervously ran 27 miles on a 15-inch ribbon before I reached

After enduring narrow roads in Tennessee and Mississippi, Randy enjoys a respite at the Alabama state line.

the Alabama state line. Hallelujah! You can't imagine my excitement when I topped a hill and saw that, beginning at the Alabama state line, the road had wide shoulders. In addition to wide shoulders, there were other novelties that Alabama had that its neighboring states did not have: mileage markers and signs telling distances to next towns. I quickly became an Alabama fan.

It rained off and on most of the day. That had become a good thing in that it keeps the temperatures cooler. Rain on!

The map listed towns on Highway 72 that I'm not sure I ever saw. No, it wasn't because of my blinding speed; but at day's end, I didn't remember seeing a couple of these: Glen, Burnsville, Luka, Oldham, Cherokee, and ended in Barton.

This day was my wife Marcy's birthday. I'm sure it was the birthday she had always dreamed of: sitting in a motor home most of the day in rainy weather, cooking dinner in cramped spaces at night, watching a TV with a tiny screen, and being with an exhausted husband. I wondered if she thought of the marriage vow she had taken many years earlier: for better or for worse. She had no idea what she was getting into, did she? Life on the road — you can't beat it!

One thing that surprised me during my weeks on the road

was the number of outstanding long-distance runners who e-mailed me, most of whom I knew only by name. Bill Schultz and Dave McGillivray had done their own cross-country runs. Mark Godale, at the time of my run, was one of the best ultra-runners in the United States and a member of the U.S. 100-kilometer team that competed internationally. Charlie Eidel had run races up to 1,000 miles. Tom Andrews had just set a U.S. 40-44 age record for the number of miles covered in a 48-hour race. Paul Stasso, Bonnie Busch, and Oklahoma's Harry Deupree and Jack Christian are all accomplished ultra-runners. Several people, like John Wood and Larry Phillips, had run numerous marathons. Long-distance runners have a certain empathy (or would that be envy?) for the long-distance undertakings of other runners.

Have you wondered how the Bunion Derby runners were faring in these recent days? After 55 days, the race had reached East St. Louis, and Peter Gavuzzi led Andy Payne by nearly two hours. During days 56 through 63, the runners ran from St. Louis to Chicago.

On days 56 through 59, Gavuzzi pushed the pace and finished either first or second for the stage on each of those days. He usually finished well ahead of Payne and had stretched his cumulative lead to about five and one-half hours. On days 60 through 63, the two runners jockeyed back and forth, and Gavuzzi's lead stood at almost exactly six hours as they reached Chicago.

The 2,386 miles covered in 63 days had taken a toll on the runners. Only 70 of the original 199 runners remained in the race. With third-place runner Johnny Salo being 34 hours behind Gavuzzi, it was certainly down to a two-man race between Gavuzzi and Payne. However, with just three weeks remaining, Gavuzzi was looking like a sure winner. The race had reached Chicago and the end of Route 66. It would now take other roads to New York.

Day 64, May 30.
Barton, AL to Wheeler, AL — 43.0 miles.
"Kidney Means"

VERY PRECISE WAS my 43-mile run this day. With the mileage markers every mile, it was easy to gauge progress all day. I started between markers 12 and 13 and ended between markers 55 and 56. I ran through household names of major metropolitan areas such as Barton, Red Rock Junction (was there a TV show about this place?), Tuscumbia, Leighton, Town Creek, North Courtland, and Wheeler.

For the past few days, I had been trying to plan out the remaining days until my anticipated finishing date. Every night, I would sit down with the maps and plot out my route and estimated miles. I had picked Saturday, June 13, two weeks from this day, as my targeted finishing date. A Saturday finish would work best for family and friends for their drive from Oklahoma to the finish at Myrtle Beach State Park in South Carolina.

I calculated that I would need to average 38.5 miles per day in order to finish on that Saturday. Since I had been averaging closer to 42 miles per day, I was confident I could make it to the ocean in two more weeks. I soon discovered that actual mileage may vary from estimated mileage.

The excitement of finishing was building as I was planning the next two weeks. However, this day brought a new concern. My journal noted "B.U. concern." My cryptic note was such that no one but me would know what it meant. B.U. stood for bloody urine.

During the latter part of the day, I darted into some trees for a bathroom stop. For the first time in my life, my urine was a dark red and somewhat painful. Knowing Marcy and my dad would worry, I elected not to tell them. However, I began imagining all kinds of possible difficulties. I thought of how disappointing it would be to come all this way only to end up in a hospital with kidney problems.

However, I thought of the e-mails that I received from Rick White, whom I had met in Edmond, Oklahoma. Rick always included this in his e-mails, "When the going gets tough, SMILE!" He promised me that one day he would tell me the background of this statement. On this day, I received the explanation.

Rick wrote, "When I starting my training for the New York City Marathon last summer, a co-worker was in his final rounds with his three-year bout with cancer. I was visiting him in the hospital about three weeks before he died, when his priest came into the room. Jerry would always smile when someone came into the room. He was lying there, thin, scraggly hair from chemo, very thin and pale, etc., with a huge SMILE. The priest commented to him, 'Jerry, every time I come in here you are smiling.' Jerry replied, 'This smile was given to me by God, and it is the one thing that cancer can't take away from me!' "

A smile and, of course, a relationship with God through His Son can never be taken away. Paul asks the question, *"Who shall separate us from the love of Christ?"* (Romans 8:35). He goes on to give the answer: nothing can! So, even with the concern over the B.U., I could SMILE this night.

We stayed all night on the parking lot of the Bethlehem Baptist Church just east of Wheeler. We must have aroused the suspicions of the locals. Soon after we had settled in for the evening, a Hillsboro police officer stopped by the church and checked us out. I guess our explanation was realistic enough. After visiting awhile, he wished us good luck as he left.

Day 65, May 31.
Wheeler, AL to Huntsville, AL — 42.0 miles.
"Sweat Roam Alabama"

EVERY DAY SEEMED to be getting hotter and more humid. Last night, the Hillsboro police officer told us you almost need oxygen masks around here during July and August. That might be an exaggeration, but I do know that at the end of May and beginning of June it was very hot and humid. After just a few miles, I could ring significant amounts of water, make that sweat, out of my clothes.

Due to the heat, I was getting started in the morning as soon as it was barely light. This morning, my watch read 5:34 when I started running. Fortunately, today was a no "B.U." day.

After running through Decatur on Highway 72, I ran over a very long, nearly two-mile bridge over the very wide Tennessee River. At the point I crossed, it made the Mississippi River at Memphis look like a creek — or "crick" as they might say around here.

The landscape had been rolling hills in western Alabama and flat through the Tennessee River valley. However, when I reached Huntsville, I knew that I had reentered the hills.

After posting this day on my website, I was to learn some geography that I will share. Sapulpan Fred Mauch e-mailed to say that the Tennessee River goes south down through Tennessee, Alabama and the corner of Mississippi. It then goes north across Tennessee and Kentucky before emptying into Kentucky Lake. It is the only known river in the northern hemisphere to flow north for a considerable distance (across two states)." See there, you did get some knowledge from this book after all.

That's not all the knowledge that Fred sent me. I also learned that an anagram is a word or phrase made by rearranging the letters of another word or phrase. Here's some examples he sent that caught my fancy:

Dormitory = Dirty Room
Desperation = A Rope Ends It
Slot Machines = Cash Lost in 'em
A Decimal Point = I'm a Dot in Place
Snooze Alarms = Alas! No More Z's
Contradiction = Accord not in it

As you can tell, I never knew what might be waiting for me when I dialed into the website after a long day on the roads.

As we spent the night in beautiful and hilly Monte Sano State Park, and as was my nightly custom, I agonized over the maps. I was discovering that actual mileage generally exceeded the estimated mileage derived from the maps. I had averaged 42.5 miles each of the last two days; yet I was still calculating that I needed to average 38.5 miles for each remaining day until June 13. Even though I was running extra miles each day, it was not reducing the amount of miles that I needed to average for each remaining day. It was to be a frustrating and recurring nightly process for the next few days.

Day 66, June 1.
Huntsville, AL to Scottsboro, AL — 43.3 miles.
"A Drinking Problem"

THIS WAS A scenic day as Highway 72 wound through the mountains between Huntsville and Scottsboro. After early morning showers, the afternoon was hot and humid; or, as I noted in my diary — the sweatiest day yet.

Most of the roads had little or no shoulder to them. Dad's diary entry for this day had the best suggestion: "Ought to introduce legislation to make every major highway have a 6-foot shoulder on each side."

The B.U. was back today. In the afternoon my urine was a bright red color and somewhat painful. Since I did not have a problem the previous day, I thought the problem had gone away. I was wrong.

I became more and more worried as the problem persisted all afternoon. To show you how worried I was, that night I told Marcy about it. As wonderful wives do, she thought it over and got right to the real problem. She said, "I don't think you're drinking enough fluids."

It had been much warmer and more humid over the past several days as compared to the cool temperatures for most of the first few weeks of the run. Also, I was averaging more miles per day. However, I had not increased by any significant amount the fluids I had been drinking.

We decided that she and Dad would meet me more often and, additionally, I would carry a water bottle between stops. Of course, I would not only carry a water bottle, but I would drink the water in it. Sure enough, much to my relief, the problem went away early the next day and never returned. I happily realized, "I am not going to the hospital with kidney failure and I will finish the run."

This night we camped in a scenic park on the Tennessee River. In my diary I called it the Duck Pond Creek Park or River. On the website I called it Goose Pond Colony Park. I assume the latter would be correct since there were plenty of geese in the park. The heat and humidity had just about cooked my goose this day.

My cousin, Steve Long, had concluded his e-mail with the admonition to: "Take care and stay away from the Kudzu." Ironically, before Steve's message, I had stopped and asked a man the name of this wild vine. In the south, there are green, ivy-looking vines that envelop and take over anything in its path. It grows rapidly and overwhelms and kills all the trees and vegetation in its path. There were times when I was plodding so slowly in the heat and humidity that I kept a wary eye on the surrounding kudzu, making sure it didn't overtake me.

11

GEORGIA ON MY MIND

Day 67, June 2.
Scottsboro, AL to Summerville, GA — 43.0 miles.
"Corny Day"

EXCITEMENT ABOUNDED AS I had Georgia on my mind! I reached the Georgia state line, thus entering the Eastern Time Zone at the 33-mile mark today. Only one state line left, the big one — South Carolina.

The views today were outstanding, but hard earned. The morning started with a long climb up Sand Mountain. There was an even bigger climb near the state line as I ascended Lookout Mountain. As big as these were, they may not hold a candle to, or match the nearby Smoky Mountains. (Read that sentence again. Don't flame out on me.)

We were the recipients of an interesting tour this morning. During one of our rest stops in front of the White Seed Company, we met the owner, Michael White. White Seed Company grows and produces popcorn in mass quantities. It sells 800 bags of popcorn PER DAY. Mr. White gave us a tour of his facilities and explained the process to us. Here was a guy who may not have made it through high school, but was a brilliant mechanical engineer. He had invented and made much of his popcorn separation equipment. It was nice people like him who added much enjoyment to the days on the road.

I wound through the mountains, passing through Heniger on Highway 40, Hammondville and Mentone on Highway 117, and Menlo on Highway 48. We spent the night in the weird James "Sloppy" Floyd State Park. Although the campgrounds were nice (and not sloppy), there was not another person in the park: no attendant and no campers. It was quiet, but a bit spooky.

It was a little depressing looking at the map this night. Four nights ago I had calculated that I needed to average 38.5 miles per day in order to finish on Saturday, June 13. I had run 42 to 43 miles each of the past four days. However, when I recalculated remaining mileage I figured I needed to average 38.9 miles for the remaining days, more than I previously thought.

Even though I had put in extra miles each day, my required daily average had actually gone up. How could that be? Who knows? My guess was that (1) map mileages were not always exact; (2) the mileage for some of the one or two-mile sections might not be shown; (3) the tenths of miles are dropped and the whole number not rounded up; and (4) sometimes it was longer across a city than it appeared on the map.

Maybe it made me feel a little better when I came up with some possible reasons. I was trying not to get discouraged, but I wasn't sure if I could keep pushing the miles in order to finish in 10 more days on a Saturday. However, my family was planning on a Saturday finish, and I felt the pressure to finish then.

In reality, I couldn't get discouraged with e-mails like this from Caryl Beard, which made me realize I had a rooting section made up of people I would never know. She wrote, "I recently moved to Texas (from Tulsa), and my internet absence left me feeling like I was missing out on your progress. You'll get a kick out of knowing that after unboxing the computer,

Only two states to go after reaching the Georgia state line. Note the water bottle — no "B.U." concern this day.

dialing up and checking e-mail after a two-week hiatus, the first website I visited was yours. I had to see how/where you were! I'm really not sure why I'm e-mailing you other than to tell you that people all over the country are interested in your progress and cheering for you. I'm not even a runner. I'm just proud of your ambition and desire to fulfill a dream."

Caryl may not have been sure why she wrote, but I knew there was an overarching purpose to hers and hundreds of other e-mails. Through God's providence and orchestrating design, many people had played a part in my journey through their encouragement, kind words, and prayer.

Day 68, June 3.

Summerville, GA to Cassville, GA — 42.0 miles.

"Unabridged Comment"

THIS WAS A day of running on small highways having little or no shoulders and meandering through rolling hills and lots of pinewood trees. I started the morning west of Summerville in northwest Georgia on Highway 48. At the junction of Highway 27, I took Highway 140 to Adairsville. Then it was south on Highway 41 to Cassville. No shoulders and plenty of heat — it reached about 95 degrees on this and the previous day.

Early in the afternoon, I ran through one of the many areas of road construction. (Does Alabama or Georgia ever complete a road project?) As I was running over the older existing bridge, there were several men working on a new adjacent bridge. Take my word, running by construction workers was generally not a pleasant thing. Construction workers tend to harass tall, skinny guys in running shorts, especially those tall, skinny runners running out in the middle of nowhere.

I had learned that with construction workers the best defense is a good offense. I would generally preempt their sarcastic remarks by hollering out as soon as they saw me, "Good morning. How are you guys doing?" That would catch them by surprise. By the time they recovered their wits, I was already on down the road.

However, on this afternoon, I decided to simply try running by them quietly and hope they didn't notice me. As I ran by, staring straight ahead, I heard one of the guys say loudly, "[Expletive deleted], I saw that guy running when I drove to work this morning!"

Against my better judgment, I looked toward the men. The worker hollered over the noise of the traffic, "You've run a long ways."

By this time, all the men had stopped working and were

staring at me. I paused, pointed behind me and then pointed forward and yelled, "Yes, sir. From Los Angeles to Myrtle Beach."

I could only imagine the looks on their faces. I could only imagine because I quickly resumed running and never looked back. Fortunately, I didn't hear any further conversation over the traffic.

At the end of today's run, we drove to a KOA campground near Cassville. The campground was off the beaten path and not easy to find. As we were relaxing in the afternoon, we were pleasantly surprised by visitors.

Friend David Pritz and his daughter Emily had driven here from our hometown of Sapulpa, Oklahoma. David had said he would help me any way he could. Since he was known for his planning abilities and he was somewhat familiar with these parts, I suggested that it would be very helpful if he could scout out the remainder of the run and determine the best way to get to Myrtle Beach State Park.

He had left Oklahoma very early in the morning and amazingly had found us in a hard-to-find campground. He would leave the following morning and go visit his brother in Atlanta. He then would head to the ocean on his scouting trip.

Day 69, June 4.
Cassville, GA to Ducktown, GA — 42.3 miles.
"Drowned Duck"

ECHOING AN OLDER song, "It's a rainy night in Georgia, a rainy night in Georgia. I feel like it's rainin' all ova da world." If you can't guess, it was a rainy afternoon. The last 10 miles were in the pouring rain; thus, it was only fitting that I would end in Ducktown.

The first six miles in the morning took me north of Cartersville (appropriate name for a Georgia town, in light of former President Jimmy Carter being from the state), where I took Highway 20 east for the rest of the day. It was not a good omen when I stopped near Cartersville to ask a man for directions to Highway 20. He looked at me and asked incredulously, "You want to run on that road?"

Sure enough, there was heavy traffic most of the day, and there were generally no shoulders and tall weeds on the side of the road. It made for a long and challenging day, topped off by all the rain in the afternoon. Marcy wrote in the diary, "The road had no shoulder and was very busy. I could say I was worried — but I didn't feel that way. I know that God is watching over Randy and has provided him with so much protection thus far that I have His sweet peace."

Though a tough running day, it was a day for humorous musings as three different things caught my eye. As I ran by the Primitive Macedonian Church, the first thing I noticed was an electric porch light on each side of the front door. How primitive was that?

Secondly, at about the 40-mile mark I ran through the little town of Free Home. As I ran down the main thoroughfare, I noticed a "For Sale" sign in front of a house. It seemed paradoxical to have a house for sale in Free Home.

Further down the street was a school building with a "Free Home School" sign on it. It seemed odd to have a "Free Home School" building. Generally, well, you know — home schools don't have buildings.

Mike Jeffries wrote an e-mail that included this observation: "I'm thoroughly enjoying reading your journal and look forward to seeing it in book format. I wonder how many people catch and appreciate your sense of humor." I don't know, Mike, but here six years later, and after the last three paragraphs, we shall see.

Friend David Tucker wrote, "Wanted to tell you how much I've enjoyed reading your daily journal and following your progress. I can't tell you how many times I've been sitting at my terminal and just burst out laughing or just chuckled to myself. It's obvious that you are still of a sound mind (can you say that about someone who decides to quit his job and run across the U.S.?) and still have your sense of humor." That parenthetical question was David's writing, though shared by many.

A.J. Sommers e-mailed this message: "I found your website while cruising the internet at my office in New Orleans. I haven't read the whole site so I'm not quite sure why you're doing this." (A.J., there were times on this challenging day that I could have read my website and not been able to tell you why I am doing this either.) A.J. went on to say, "But, nonetheless, as a runner myself and more importantly, a born-again Christian, I pray that the Lord will continue to bless your 'mission' to cross the U.S.A."

Oh yes, the Bunion Derby! Some big developments were taking place on days 64 through 69. We had last left the runners in Chicago, where Gavuzzi had a six-hour lead over Payne after 63 days.

After a relatively short run of 28.4 miles from Chicago to Gary, the runners were subjected to a 66.2-mile run from Gary to Mishawaka, Illinois. Payne managed to stay with Gavuzzi and they finished together in 11 hours and 24 minutes. Two additional runners dropped out on this long segment, leaving 63 remaining out of the 199 starters.

On days 66 and 67, Payne and Gavuzzi finished together. However, a major development took place on day 68 when Gavuzzi reported at the start line that the tooth that had been bothering him for some time was now abscessed. However, he decided to try to make it through the 44.9-mile segment from Butler, Illinois to Waseon, Ohio. Perhaps sensing that the tide might be turning, Payne ran hard and finished the segment in second place in a time of 6 hours and 58 minutes.

Much like Payne had done with the tonsillitis, Gavuzzi struggled all day, finishing the day well behind the leaders. Although Payne's tonsillitis had gotten better, Gavuzzi's infected tooth was even more inflamed at the end of the day.

On day 69, the runners had to cover 60 miles from Waseon to Freemont, Ohio. Gavuzzi gamely started the run, but dropped out during the day. At day's end, Oklahoma's Andy Payne held a nearly insurmountable 24-hour lead over second place Johnny Salo. Of course, the lead was only insurmountable if Payne could stay healthy and finish every day's segment.

Day 70, June 5.
Ducktown, GA to Russell, GA — 44.6 miles.
"Getting Cross"

RAIN AND MORE rain. There was something about that Ducktown, and I was going to be glad to leave it behind. I started running at 5:55 a.m., and it started raining very hard five minutes later. It was miserable running conditions for most of the day: a combination of heavy rain, heavy traffic and generally no shoulder. The good thing is that the rain kept the temperatures very mild. I felt very blessed to complete 44.6 miles for the day.

School was not quite finished for the summer in many of the towns in the South. As I was running through Cummins in the morning in the heavy rain, a Cummins school bus drove past. Many of the young children on the bus had their faces pressed against the window, staring at this strange man running down the road in the pouring rain. They knew their moms would never let them do that — as fun as it seemed. I could just imagine the bus driver pointing at me and telling those children, "You all kids be sure and get a good learnin' cause you don't wanna end up like that fella."

Running in the rain was cool, but shortly after the bus passed by, I lost my cool. I was running down a Cummins sidewalk in the heavy rain and reached an intersection. I saw a car approaching the side-street intersection, but since he had a stop sign I assumed I had plenty of time to make it across the street safely. What I didn't realize was his intentions of speeding up and running the stop sign in order to take advantage of a perceived break in traffic on the highway. I was about halfway across the intersection and he was almost to me when we both realized that neither of us was planning on stopping. We both then stopped abruptly.

We both paused and looked at each other. Thinking he was going to yield the right-of-way to a poor, drowning pedestrian, I started to resume my crossing. As I took my first step, he hit the accelerator again, almost hitting me with his right front bumper. However, by this time the break in traffic was gone and he had to stop immediately to keep from pulling in front of an oncoming car.

Now he was stopped right in front on me, blocking the street, as I stood a foot away from his passenger side front door. Steam was starting to rise from me as anger was getting the best of me. I slapped the roof of his car and ran around to the driver's side. (I ran around behind the car — I'm not completely insane!)

Fortunately or unfortunately, he still had not been able to pull out on the highway. I ran up to the driver-side window (which fortunately or unfortunately was closed due to the rain), glared in, and yelled, "IDIOT!" I might have yelled it more than once; but, thankfully, he ignored me until he got his opening in the traffic and pulled away.

As I resumed running down the sidewalk, I was shaking from the close encounter with the bumper of the car and the anger of the moment. Then I burst into laughing as I thought, "Now wait a minute. I left a good job to run across the country. I'm running down the sidewalk in a downpour in Cummins, Georgia, 1,000 miles from home. This guy is in a dry car, in a hurry to get to a real job. Who's the idiot here?"

However, the close call with the car made me once again realize how God had protected me on the run. I shudder to think of all the trucks and cars that sped by just a few feet or less from me. One time in particular stands out. I was running against the traffic on a narrow two-lane road with no shoulders in Georgia. I stepped off the road to let an approaching car go by me. I then started to step back on the road, but, at the last moment, glanced behind me over my right shoulder. A car in the process of passing a car had swerved over into the lane that I was just about to step into. Thank the Lord, I stopped just short of stepping in front of the car. It was probably going at least 70 mph as it flew by, just inches away. I learned to always look for passing cars coming up from behind me.

Back to the run. After Dad and Marcy let me off to start the run in Ducktown, they drove to the next town to find a grocery store. In the rain and darkness, I did not see the motor home at the store when I ran by and they didn't see me. After awhile, they decided I must have gone by, so they drove on up the road — but not far enough to catch me before they turned back around and headed toward where I had started. Dad wrote in his diary, "We really worried and prayed that God would let us find him. Finally we just decided to go forward till we found him. That was almost 20 miles he had run. I was elated when I saw him because the weather was horrible." A crew's job often is more difficult than running. I was in my own world oblivious to the anxiety being suffered by Dad and Marcy.

On the route today, Marcy pointed out a volunteer fire department building with the following sign: "New _embers Needed." Either someone had stolen the "M" from the sign or that town had a clever fireman.

In Winder, a red sports car full of college-age students came down the street toward me. Since the car was full of both boys and girls, I braced for another drive-by shouting. Sure enough, one of the boys hung out the window and yelled, "Hey, buddy, get you a bike; it's faster."

Now think about this. Remember the story I started the book

with: the five-year-old boy in Chandler, Oklahoma told me to "Buy you a car!" Now, here's a carload of college students, and the best solution they can come up with is to get a bike. Who's smarter: the college students or the five-year-old boy in Chandler, Oklahoma?

Friend and scout David Pritz returned from traveling the route to Myrtle Beach. News was not good. The remaining trip would be mostly on roads with no shoulder and heavy traffic. Of course, the good news was that I only had a few days remaining.

After looking at the options, we picked a route that would eventually take us to Highway 501 and Myrtle Beach. We estimated 315 miles to the edge of the water — low tide, of course. Having run 300 miles the past seven days, I was now confident that I could finish on the Saturday I had planned, which gave me eight more running days.

Day 71, June 6.
Russell, GA to Lexington, GA — 45.0 miles.
"Here's the Pitch"

NAVIGATING DOWN A series of small highways, I ran two miles on South 53 to 316/29 before I "bulldogged" my way around Athens and the University of Georgia on Highway 78. I continued on 78 through Crawford and Lexington.

It was a cloudy and cooler day, making for a nice respite from the increasingly hot and humid weather. Of all the states that I ran through, I concluded that Georgia easily led in drive-by shoutings.

A black sports car with two teenage boys drove by three times, each time swerving toward me while hollering out the window. However, I was prepared and ready for the third time. Since they seemed to have the same sense as the many dogs I had to ward off on the roads, I figured I would try a familiar ploy. I picked up a baseball-sized rock, and when they swerved toward me this time, I reverted back to my little-league pitching days. I wound up and gave them my best fastball throwing motion as though a rock was about to proceed through their windshield. I had no intention of letting go of the rock, but they didn't know that. They quickly swerved away from me while ducking in the car. Fortunately, they also responded to my challenge just like most dogs, by retreating and not coming back.

As I ran through one rural area, I saw several handwritten signs along the highway that read "Fly in." Obviously there was a small airfield nearby. It just puzzled me as to why someone would have "fly in" signs on the side of the highway.

There were not many shoulders on the highways, and the traffic was heavy most of the time. I often longed for the wide-open spaces of the western states. However, only 270 miles remained to be covered over the last seven days.

I came to realize from various e-mails that many people were running across the United States vicariously through me. Tara Browning wrote from Memphis, "I am currently injured and have not been able to run for a couple of weeks, so am living vicariously through you!" I thanked Tara and apologized for my not-so-nice assessment of my run through her hometown.

On my website, I had mentioned the 1928 Bunion Derby several times, particularly earlier in the run. I received an interesting e-mail from Aaron Currier of Salem, Oregon, who had started doing his own research on that race. He wrote, "I recently met RP 'Abe' Allen, who had competed in the 1928 Bunion Derby — he's 93 now. Also, my grandfather, who died in the 1940s, finished 16th — Allan D. Currier from Grants Pass, Oregon. Abe and I have numerous newspaper clippings, the original 1928 program, and about 20 photos. I am looking for more!"

Day 72, June 7.
Lexington, GA to Lincolnton, GA — 43.0 miles.
"Shelf Starter"

A FTER A COUPLE of rainy days, this was a nice, cool morning. I ran through several small towns, as described with some word play on my website: no one hollered at me in Rayle, it was a peaceful run through Celeste; I capitolized on a shortcut through Washington; and I had the luxury of a good run through Lincolnton. You may need to read this paragraph again.

It was a very enjoyable day of seeing several Southern plantations and many antebellum homes. Marcy taught me that word. I was going to say "those old, huge two-story colonial homes with the big, tall columns in front." I guess it's shorter to say antebellum, if you know what that means — but I didn't. The spring beauty made for a scenic run.

Downtown Washington was filled with history, particularly Civil War era history. Washington was the site of the last cabinet meeting of the Confederacy where the vote was taken to dissolve the Confederacy. There were old buildings dating back to the late 1700s. We toured the Smyrna Methodist Church, which had been established in 1786. I also explored a few cemeteries and found birth dates going back to the 1790s and many death dates in the 1850s and 1860s.

Not only was the scenery wonderful, but the people we met in eastern Georgia were very friendly. And, of course, you have to love that Southern accent. The waitress in the restaurant in which we ate the previous evening had quite the Southern drawl. As we were leaving she told us, "Ba y'all."

Later in the day, a nice gentleman pulled up beside me in his car and said, "You must be training for the Boston marathon. I saw you by my house near the airport in Washington this morning."

"That's not exactly what I'm doing," I replied. When I told

him what I was doing, he asked how many miles I was running each day. When he heard I was averaging 39 miles per day, he shook his head and said, "That's one and a half marathons, each and every day." He kept shaking his head as he wished me well.

Speaking of nice folks, a wonderful act of kindness was extended to us on this day, a Sunday. This was an example of our sovereign God providing help at the exact time it was needed by having the right person come into our life. We will forever be grateful to John Wayne Johnson of Lincolnton, Georgia.

This particular day, Dad and Marcy encountered the first major problem with the motor home. After one of our pit stops, the starter would not engage. Dad had to get underneath and tap on the starter before it would start the engine.

After meeting me for a quick break, Dad drove the remaining five miles into Lincolnton, our planned stopping point for the day. He found a parking place at a point of interest just off the highway, crawled under the motor home, and began examining the starter. Mr. Johnson stopped to see if he was having problems and whether he could help.

After Dad told him about our adventure and the starter problem, Mr. Johnson told Dad, "We have an auto parts store here in town; but, of course, it's closed on Sunday. However, I know the owner. Let's go to his house and see if he would happen to have a new starter down at the store."

Mr. Johnson drove Dad to the owner's house (actually, Mr. Johnson drove his car — Dad was just in the car) and introduced him to Hiller Wright, owner of R & W Auto Parts store. Dad told him what we were doing and asked him about a starter for the motor home. Mr. Wright said he had one at the store and if they would wait just a moment, he would get his keys and follow them to the store.

After they drove downtown, Mr. Wright opened his store and sold Dad a starter for a fair and reasonable price. Mr. Johnson drove Dad back to the motor home, where, by this time, I had happily finished for the day.

Dad and I both offered Mr. Johnson money for his gas and time. He refused and said the only payment he wanted was for us to return the favor to someone else in need. I have always remembered Mr. Johnson and "the payment" that he wanted. I have helped others, and when they thanked me and asked what they could do for me, I told them about Mr. Johnson and how he had helped us. I asked for the same payment that he did.

Not wanting to work on the starter on the side of the road, we decided to drive on down the road to Elijah Clark State Park for the evening. Thankfully, the old starter came through one more time and we headed to the park. There we met a very nice Christian couple who was overseeing the campground. Don and his wife were wonderful hosts.

Once there and parked for the night, Dad began working on the starter. He discovered he didn't have the right tools to make the change. We decided that if God would grant one more start tomorrow morning, Dad and Marcy would drive into McCormick, the next town, and try to find a garage that would install it.

Day 73, June 8.
Lincolnton, GA to Saluda, SC — 45.4 miles.
"Cool Runnings"

LEAVING THE STARTER problem to God and trusting Him was not easy that night. After a night of wondering and praying, early the next morning Dad turned the key. We praised the Lord when the starter engaged and the engine started. We drove down the road and found a pay phone for my Monday morning ritual of calling John Erling at KRMG radio in Tulsa for a live interview. This was the last Monday interview, but he asked if I would call when I reached the finish on Saturday.

Dad and Marcy dropped me off where I had stopped the

previous day and drove two miles on down the road to the South Carolina state line, the last state line I would cross. They did not turn off the motor home engine; it was running and they wanted it to stay that way until they found a garage. After I ran across a narrow bridge over the Savannah River and reached the state line at the east end of the bridge, we took a few of the customary (but last) state-line pictures. Afterward, they left and drove the seven miles on to McCormick, South Carolina.

When I later ran into downtown McCormick, Marcy was hurriedly walking up to the main street from a side street, where we reached the intersection at the same time. She was very relieved to catch me before I made it past this point. Dad had found a garage a few blocks off the main street, and a very helpful mechanic was installing the new starter. Marcy and I walked to the garage, and soon the mechanic was finished and the motor home was as good as new. Well, I guess an old motor home can't be as good as new, but it did start the first time, every time after that. We were so thankful for a very nice mechanic.

In a nice break from the normal weather, it was unseasonably cool all day. The television news said that Colombia's low temperature of 52 degrees was nearly a record for this day. It was delightful to run through Sumter National Forest with light traffic on a relatively cool day.

I was serenaded today by a boy on a porch playing "This Old Man" over and over on his trombone. I could hear him for blocks before I reached his house and for blocks afterwards. Since the miles were piling up and my body growing weary and feeling old, he must have been playing just for me.

In a nice break from the cramped quarters of the motor home, Marcy and I got a room at the Saluda Inn in Saluda, South Carolina. Dad was worried about someone breaking into the motor home if someone wasn't in it, so he opted to keep the fort and stay in the quiet motor home. Just five more days to go!

Day 74, June 9.
Saluda, SC to West Colombia, SC — 39.4 miles.
"A Foot Shoulder"

SCOUT DAVID PRITZ was right when he said he didn't think that South Carolina believed in shoulders on the roads. As I was running through three miles of road construction this day, I wanted to stop and ask the construction workers if the new road would have a shoulder, or if they had ever considered adding one. However, I didn't want to disturb the men who were working, and I didn't want to draw the wrath of the much larger group of men who were standing and watching the other men work.

My question about a shoulder on the new highway was soon answered when I reached a completed portion of the new highway. Right there on the side of the new highway was a brand-spanking new shoulder, all of 12 inches wide. It's hard to complain in that it sure beats nothing, but 12 inches? C'mon, South Carolina, give us a little more space.

I was sometimes asked what I thought about when I was running all alone. Geoff Jones wrote, "One thing I was wondering ... what on earth do you think about when you're staring at that long road ahead of you each day? My guess would be 'What on earth am I doing here?' " There were many times on the shoulderless roads of Tennessee, Georgia, and South Carolina when that was my exact thought: "What on earth am I doing here?"

I wrote on the website about enjoying running more in the wide-open spaces of the West versus the more crowded East. Former co-worker Cathy Marker wrote in her e-mail, "I wonder if you started from the East and went West, would you enjoy the East more. Maybe, you should try it, just to see! A scientific study!" Gee, wonderful suggestion, but no thanks, Cathy.

One of the enjoyable things about spending many early mornings on the road is the sighting of animals. I saw deer in many areas of the country. There were also antelope, rabbits, numerous squirrels, and this morning a beautiful gray fox ambled across the road about 20 yards in front of me.

I cut the day's mileage a bit shorter this day. I was getting close to downtown Colombia, and the afternoon rush hour traffic was starting. Additionally, I was feeling a little more "beat up" each day. Running more miles per day the previous few days, together with more heat and humidity, was taking a toll. However, with just four days to go, the aches and pains were but a *"light affliction, which is but for a moment"* (II Corinthians 4:17).

The aches and pains of running were light, particularly when compared to the fatigue and difficulty of being the crew, especially for Dad. He had the jobs of continually negotiating narrow, busy roads in a large motor home and being responsible for the repairs such as to the starter and the holding tank. Those things coupled with being away from home for 10 out of the last 11 weeks made for a difficult last two weeks of the run for him. Of course, the biggest difficulty was being away from his wife of 48 years for the last 18 days of the journey, easily the longest they had ever been apart. Dad mentioned more than once in his diary what all of us thought at one time or the other: the motor home was getting smaller and smaller.

We stayed in the Barnyard RV Park, right behind the Barnyard Flea Market just west of downtown Colombia. This was the largest flea market we had ever seen. There were five buildings and each seemed to be about one-half mile in length. We were glad we were "fleaing" early the next morning and would not be there on a Friday through Sunday when it was open.

12

BEACH ASSAULT

Day 75, June 10.
West Colombia, SC to Sumter, SC — 53.0 miles.
"All Scene Gestures"

LEAVING THE RV Park at 5:15 a.m., I was planning a long day; but I had no idea of just how long it was to be. By 6 a.m. I had crossed the Congaree River into downtown Colombia and was running in front of the state capitol. Soon I was running headlong into the morning rush hour traffic. Fortunately, during this stretch the highway had a nice shoulder.

It was on this stretch of road with a shoulder that I noticed a small monument built to honor the man who was responsible for building this road, as well as 1,100 miles of other state roads. Sure, that made sense! Put the monument on the rare stretch of road that had a shoulder! I had to wonder how much more they would have honored this gentleman had he included shoulders on more than just 17 miles of his 1,100 miles of roads.

At about mid-morning and after the nice shoulder ended, heavy, drenching rains and frequent lightning came. I could only imagine what drivers thought of this man running down the grassy side of the highway in the pouring rain and crackling lightning, out away from civilization. So, I decided to have a good time with my highway antics. Here is a sample of a few of my highway gestures that I occasionally used to entertain motorists as I ran across the country:

(1) **"Windshield wiper" gesture** — Looping my arm up from behind and over the top of my head, I extended the side of my hand down the middle of my forehead and between my eyes. Then I moved my hand back and forth in front of my eyes like it was a windshield wiper. Of course, a heavy rain is the best time to pull this gesture out of the bag.

(2) **"Please, just a little space" gesture** — If a driver would not move over a little and share the highway, I raised my arms in front of me and held my hands about 12 inches apart as if I were begging that he would spare just a small portion of "his" or "her" highway.

(3) **"After you" gesture** — Or if they would not yield a portion of the highway, I stepped off the road, bowed and extended my arm as if I was letting them enter a room before me. "Here, you go ahead and take the road, all of it."

(4) **"Flying off and on the road" gesture** — Or I would extend my arms straight out to each side and pretend to be an airplane, flying off the side of the road and flying back on after they passed (knowing they were looking into their rear view mirror, wondering what the heck was that).

(5) **"Flagman" gesture** — If the driver was driving too fast, I stepped off the road and waved my hand back and forth and up and down like a NASCAR flagman, as though the driver had just taken the checkered flag.

These gestures are not patented. You are welcome to try these or develop your own derivatives that work better for you.

One recommendation is that you don't use these in your own neighborhood for obvious reasons. I always felt more comfortable using them when I was many miles from my home area.

Can you imagine seeing a grown man doing these things in the heavy rain on the side of a busy highway miles from the nearest civilization? Since the drivers were already wondering about this strange guy running down the road, I just figured that I would really give them something to ponder. I enjoyed trying to make something fun out of something that was ludicrous, not to mention dangerous.

You may have noted that I ran 53 miles this day (at least 53 miles), which was entirely too much. Running that many miles wasn't by design. It was to be my only day of running over 45 miles.

I reached Sumter at the 45-mile mark. Contrary to my crew's wishes, I decided to run two extra miles in order to reach the Highway 15 intersection. Running against the traffic (or opposite the side that you would drive on) has its disadvantages, especially on a divided highway. The road signs are all on the opposite side of the road from the runner.

Somehow I missed the sign and the correct turn that would have gotten me to the Highway 15 intersection, which would have skirted around town. I mistakenly took Highway 76, the wrong road, which took me to downtown Sumter. When I reached downtown, I realized that I had missed the correct road. I had to stop several times and ask directions on how to get through town and to Highway 378 on the east side of town.

Asking directions in Sumter was an adventure in itself. I approached a man pumping gas into his car at a convenience store and asked him how to get to Highway 378. After he said a few words, none of which I understood, I kindly thanked him and took off — probably in the wrong direction. Fortunately, I was able to understand the next person I asked — and the one after that — and the one after that.

Of course, as I was wandering around downtown Sumter, Dad and Marcy had no idea as to where I had disappeared. All they could do was keep driving the correct roads. Eventually I made my way to Highway 378, where I was found by my crew. The extra two miles turned into an estimated extra eight miles and made for a long day.

Our closest encounter to a serious motor home accident came while Dad and Marcy stopped to pick me up. A truck moving a house came down the road and nearly hit the side of the motor home. You can't image how very thankful I was to get off the highway and call it a day, a long day, a very long day.

Day 76, June 11.
Sumter, SC to past Lake City, SC — 40.0 miles.
"The Final A Salt"

IT WAS PREDICTABLE. After 53 miles the previous day, this day was more of a struggle than usual. The body creaked, groaned, and protested getting started in the morning. It felt as though I was coaxing it onward and doing so on pure adrenaline. The heat and humidity were threatening to sap the adrenaline. I felt as though I had started my finishing kick, well, finishing shuffle, a few days ago and I was just trying to maintain it to the finish.

As I had written earlier, one of the joys of the run across the country was meeting some very nice people. As Dad was stopped alongside the highway waiting for me, Mr. Emerson Hayes stopped to see if he needed help. Mr. Hayes was on his way to church on this Thursday morning in order to continue working on an addition the congregation was making to the building.

Similar to Dad, Mr. Hayes was a devout Christian, as well as a devoted family man. He had a noticeable peace and joy in his life. Just like Dad, he had three sons and enjoyed talking about them. Dad and Mr. Hayes had a lengthy conversation, just as though they were friends who hadn't seen each other in years.

Mr. Hayes wanted a phone number so that he could call a few days later and get a final report on the finish of the run. Sure enough, Mr. Hayes called to check on us after we arrived back home. For years afterwards, Dad and Mr. Hayes exchanged Christmas cards and occasional letters. Recently, Mrs. Hayes wrote Dad to inform him that her husband had gone to be with the Lord. Mr. Hayes had touched our lives and I'm sure the lives of countless others.

Later in the day, we stopped and took pictures at our first Myrtle Beach road sign: "Myrtle Beach 81," which meant 81 plus some amount of miles to go. The soil was getting sandier, and the biggest hills on this day were two overpasses. I spotted an occasional palm tree and kept sniffing the air hoping to smell salt water.

We always noticed the unusual church names. Today, we saw the Free Will Baptist Pentecostal Faith Church. How do they get all that on their church bulletins? Or maybe two churches share the same building.

Sniffing the air sounds silly, but you can't believe the continual excitement that was building, knowing that in two more days I would reach the goal. We spent the night at Security Inn in Lake City. I never saw a lake in the area, so I pretended it was named after the huge "lake" that lay 60 miles ahead of me. We enjoyed calling all the family back home and finding out their plans to drive all Friday night and join us for the finish. So much excitement! Would I be able to sleep? The more appropriate question was would I be able to get up in the morning?

I figured I had 58 miles left: 40 to be run on Friday and a short day of 18 miles on Saturday morning. I was determined to finish 10 a.m. (EST) which is 7 a.m. (PST), nearly the same time I had started exactly 11 weeks ago.

Before I conclude my run, here's the final chapter to the Bunion Derby story. If you remember back to day 69, Peter

At last! Randy reaches the first road sign showing Myrtle Beach, SC, the journey's destination.

Gavuzzi, who had led much of the race, dropped out due to an abscessed tooth. That left Andy Payne with a 24-hour lead over Johnny Salo. Payne simply had to stay healthy and finish each day in a decent time.

Payne did indeed stay healthy by running conservatively over the last 15 days. On day 84, the final day of the Bunion Derby, the runners ran a few miles to reach New York's original (not the current) Madison Square Garden sports center, and then 20 miles inside the Garden. The race had covered 3,423 miles, and Andy Payne had finished 15-1/2 hours ahead of runner-up Johnny Salo. Of the 199 starters in Los Angeles, 55 had finished the race in New York.

Andy Payne had become a national hero. He was flown to Washington, D.C. where he was introduced in the House of Representatives and later met the President.

After much concern as to whether the runners would receive their prize money, Payne did receive his $25,000 first prize.

He returned to Oklahoma, bought a new car and helped his father pay off the farm mortgage. Unlike many of the other top Bunion Derby runners, Payne would soon retire from running and never race again. In 1934 he ran for the office of the Clerk of the Supreme Court of Oklahoma, which he won easily. He would be reelected every four years and serve in that position for a total of 36 years. One other noteworthy thing took place shortly after he returned to Oklahoma as Bunion Derby champion. To complete his pre-race dreams, he married his high school teacher, Vivian.

Day 77, June 12.
Past Lake City, SC to Conway, SC — 42.7 miles.
"Oh, Can You See"

FEELING THE EFFECTS of the miles and the sun, I struggled through the stifling heat this day. I finished just past Conway where the high temperature reached 97 degrees. The running conditions and heavy traffic made for a difficult day, though bearable, and almost enjoyable, due to the pending finish.

The last three miles of the day were heading southeast out of Conway on Highway 501. There were no shoulders, only tall, sometimes knee-deep, weeds growing next to the highway. The heavy traffic often yielded little space to someone who was very much out of place running on this road.

The heat and miserable running conditions kept me busy with my own conversations throughout the day, which went like this:

(1)   To the clouds on the horizon, "I bet you are overlooking the ocean; I will be there soon."

(2)   To the many planes that flew overhead, "I bet you can see the ocean; I will be there soon."

(3)   To white birds flying overhead, "I bet you can see the ocean; I will be there soon."

Do you detect a pattern? Sounds like a one-track mind, huh? I told you; it was a very hot, humid day with precious little shade. The cumulative miles had taken a toll, and it seemed as though I was running on empty for most of the day. The constant sweating was making it difficult to keep hydrated. The difficult day was similar to challenging situations in life, where the thought of the finish keeps us plowing onward.

Roger Fox had asked in an e-mail, "Any new grand dreams, like running across Europe, China, or Russia?" My simple answer after this journey, "No, Roger, over and out!"

At about the time I finished for the day and settled in at the Ramada Limited in Conway, two carloads of my family were heading out of Sapulpa, Oklahoma. They planned to drive all night and reach Myrtle Beach State Park before my 10 a.m. projected finish. Dad, Marcy, and I worried and prayed often for their safety on the road.

Friends Jerry and Sue Neil sent an e-mail this day that said, "Please know that at 10 a.m. all of us back here in Tulsa will face the east and say a prayer of thankfulness for Randy and his family." As Dad, Marcy, and I thought of all the dangers that we had faced on the road, our hearts were filled with gratitude to God as we tried to sleep this night.

Day 78, June 13.
Conway, SC to Myrtle Beach State Park, SC — 16.6 miles.
"Beach Party"

EXCITED AS I was, somehow I was able to get a decent night's sleep. The whole trip had been one long dream. After 11 weeks of running, it felt even more like a dream to be getting up, knowing I had only a 16-mile run ahead of me. Then, it would be over.

The previous night, Robin Smith, a reporter for the *Myrtle Beach Sun* newspaper, had contacted me and asked for an interview Saturday morning. Sure enough, at 6 a.m. he knocked on our door.

After the interview, Robin accompanied us to the convenience store where I had finished the previous day. He and Marcy took some pictures before I took off. As we were taking pictures along the side of road, I stepped back and stepped right into a deep ditch that had standing water. As I was falling, I thought, "2,898 miles down, 16 miles to go, and I break my ankle taking pictures." When we all realized I was uninjured, we shared a big laugh about the thought of getting injured in this way on the last morning of the run.

At 7 a.m. I began the final portion of my run. This would give me three hours to complete the remaining 16.6 miles. For the first part of the run, I kept watching for the arrival of the two vehicles from back home. Suddenly at about 8:50 a.m., and with yelling voices and blaring horns, they drove past on the other side of the divided highway. The feeling of hearing and seeing them, and knowing they had made it safely, was the most wonderful feeling that I had experienced on the run — to that point. It would have been a hollow finish without family and friends with whom to share the thrill.

They stopped down the road at Third Street and waited for me at an auto parts store. The battery was going bad on Wayne's car, and it was by God's blessing they had made it all night without more problems. It was a happy reunion since I had not seen most of them since I had left Sapulpa five weeks earlier.

After a few minutes and a new battery, they headed for Myrtle Beach State Park. I felt as though I was running on air as I wound my way through Myrtle Beach and toward the state park. The last three miles to the park were the longest three miles of the whole run. It seemed as though I would never get to the park entrance.

Waiting at the park entrance were Dad, son Justin, daughter Nicole, and nephews Sam and Daniel, ready to run the last mile

Randy, carrying the United States flag, reaches the Atlantic Ocean at Myrtle Beach State Park.

with me. They also had the one thing I had requested for the finish: a flag of the United States of America.

It was with a combination of exhilaration and relief that I ran through a crowded Myrtle Beach State Park. Hundreds of people must have been scratching their heads as our small band ran through the park with the American flag.

There's always an anticipation and excitement to seeing the ocean. However, the ocean never looked better than it did this time. An incredible feeling of accomplishment came over me as the ocean came into view and I thought "ocean to ocean."

Do you remember the start back at Santa Monica Beach and the shoes I had worn for that occasion? My grandfather had died, and I started the journey in his old, worn-out Adidas shoes as a tribute to him. When I reached the parking lot at Myrtle Beach State Park, I changed into his old shoes for the big finish. He would not have understood "why" someone would want to run across the country, but he would have understood the perseverance that it takes.

As I arrived at the beach, I was surprised to find a television reporter for Myrtle Beach's Channel 13 waiting for me. Apparently the newspaper reporter had notified the television station of the story. An interview was about the last thing I wanted to do at that moment. I had to remind myself that after 11 weeks of running, I should not mind taking a few minutes to do a short interview. However, I could hardly wait to finish the preliminaries and get in the water.

After a few minutes, it was time to run the remaining few yards down the beach, descend a few wooden steps, and finish the long-anticipated run with a dive into the water. The feelings of dreams realized and completed are something that can never be put into words. How do you describe marrying the love of your life or witnessing the birth of your child? Some things in life are so wonderful that you just want to soak up every minute of the celebration.

If you remember the start, I had filled two plastic milk jugs with Pacific Ocean water before I had started 11 weeks earlier. Once I had splashed into the Atlantic, we retrieved the two bottles,

Randy pours some Pacific Ocean water, gathered near Santa Monica Pier, into the Atlantic Ocean at Myrtle Beach State Park.

and with a joyful ceremony I poured one jug of Pacific water into the Atlantic. Indeed, there was no chemical reaction, and the different waters seemed to coexist peacefully. I filled the empty jug with Atlantic water. Now I had one jug of Pacific water and one jug of Atlantic water. Don't ask me why I performed this ritual. All I know is that when we got back home, I transferred the water from the milk jugs into glass jars — which I still have as keepsakes from my run.

After a few minutes of celebrating, I made my last call back to Tulsa's KRMG radio station. We did a live interview over the sound of the wind and waves, as I tried to explain the excitement of having just finished. I hope they heard me.

Those who were part of the joyous celebration were my wife Marcy; my children Heather, Justin, and Nicole; Dad; Mom; brother Wayne and his sons, Daniel and Ryan; brother Craig and son Samuel; and friends Ben and Kay Anglin. I will be forever indebted to them and the sacrifice they made to be a part of the run.

We all spent several hours on the beach, trying to soak up the last bit of excitement and memories. Occasionally, I would just sit in the sand by myself and try to comprehend traveling 2,914 miles on foot in 11 weeks. It had gone so much better and faster than I could have ever dreamed. Based on averaging an anticipated 32 miles per day, before the run I had forecast that I would reach Myrtle Beach on June 29. Taking out the two off-days, I ended up averaging about 39 miles per day, reaching the finish 16 days earlier than expected.

As I sat on the beach, I was humbled and honored that God had so richly blessed me in enabling me to experience an incredible dream over an 11-week period. On March 30, the third day of the run, Roger Fox had prophetically e-mailed me, stating "Well, the dream finally is becoming a reality! ... No matter the result, you will return from this a different person than when you stood on the beach Saturday." Roger was right.

Though I had finished the run, I had a sense that the dream would never completely end. Andy Payne's dream never ended. For 76-plus years, it has captured the imagination of others and inspired them to undertake their dreams. I hope and pray *Running with Payne* provides inspiration to persevere in whatever dreams and challenges you face in life for God's glory.

POSTSCRIPT

THREE MONTHS AFTER finishing my run, I was thrilled to be invited to speak at the unveiling of a life-size statue of Andy Payne. The Heritage Association in Andy Payne's hometown of Foyil, Oklahoma had raised the funds for the statue that was placed in Foyil City Park on historic Route 66. At the unveiling ceremony, it was an honor to meet Payne's widow, Vivian Payne, and their children. The picture below was taken at that ceremony.

Randy standing next to Andy Payne's widow, Vivian Payne, at the ceremony unveiling the statue of Andy Payne in Foyil, Oklahoma.

The 11 weeks of running across the country truly had been living out a dream, but it was soon back to reality. One of life's realities is the need for income. After spending a few relaxing weeks with my wife and children, I worked as a teacher's assistant during the 1998-1999 school year. That allowed me to take a few college classes in counseling while I tried to decide what direction to take. I could find my way across the country, but wasn't sure where I was headed vocationally.

After nine months of teacher's assistant pay, reality number two became apparent. A person can't continue to spend more than they make. Soon the Lord provided a good job at CCI Corporation, and it was back into the exciting reality of accounting and finance.

I'm sometimes asked what long-term effects the run had on me. Physically, after taking several weeks off to recuperate, I was soon back into long-distance running. In March 1999, I ran one of my best 50-mile trail races. However, that was to prove to be the last long-distance hurrah to date.

I was surprised at how my recovery (or lack thereof) paralleled that of David Horton, who had written a book, *A Quest for Adventure,* about both his Appalachian Trail run and his cross-country run in the Trans America Footrace in 1995. He, too, had run a good 50-mile race shortly after finishing his cross-country run. He wrote of how he then struggled for months after that race, being injured and not able to run very well.

For me, all of the long-distance miles, coupled with advancing age and knee surgery, made for sporadic training for the four years following that last 50-mile race. In retrospect, I probably returned to long-distance running too quickly. In recent months, I once again tried to learn to set aside my fascination with long-distance running and to enjoy training for, and participating in, the shorter local running races. However, the lure of long-distance running always overtakes me, and once again I have begun running some 20+-mile training runs and dreaming of another 50- or 100-mile race.

One effect the cross-country run has had on me is to appreciate the accomplishment of others. Having tasted the enjoyment of planning and accomplishing a dream has given me an understanding of the joy that others experience when accomplishing a major dream or task. I always smile when I hear about the dreams and accomplishments of others.

However, the greatest effect on me has been an enduring awe of God's blessings. In Isaiah 46:9, God says, *"Remember the former things of old, for I am God, and there is no other; I am God and there is none like Me."* I often think back over my cross-country run and marvel at how God strengthened, protected, and blessed me. It's been nearly seven years and the amazement and appreciation of God's blessings have continued to grow.

That leads to the acronym that is contained within the book and that was mentioned in the Preface. Did you figure it out? Take pen and paper and write down the bold large first letter of each one of the 78 daily accounts. If there is not a large bold first letter, that day represents a space between words. The message contained in the acronym is the most important message that could be communicated.

The joy of accomplishing dreams, such as running across the country, may fade as the years pass, but the joy that comes from knowing Jesus Christ as Savior never fades, but grows over time. I pray that God blesses you in the difficult challenges of life as you trust in the Him, the Source of all hope and encouragement.

Randy speaking at the Andy Payne statue dedication ceremony.

Andy Payne's widow, Vivian Payne, with her son and grandson, removes the covering from the Andy Payne statue.

Appendix I

TRANSCONTINENTAL RUNS

LISTED ON THE next page is the daily mileage for Randy Ellis' solo transcontinental run in 1998, as compared to the 1928 Bunion Derby daily mileage. The Bunion Derby statistics were compiled from books and articles about the race. I have found two books written about the Bunion Derby. *The Bunion Derby — Andy Payne and the Transcontinental Footrace* was written by James H. Thomas, a professor of American Studies at Wichita State University. From what I understand, the book is no longer in print, but was published by Southwestern Heritage Books, Inc. in Oklahoma City, Oklahoma, in 1980 — ISBN 0-86546-017-5.

The other book, *From L.A. to New York, From New York to L.A.,* was written by Harry Berry in England. Berry was a friend of Peter Gavuzzi, who led much of the 1928 Bunion Derby before dropping out with an abscessed tooth. This book also incledes an account of the 1929 race from New York to Los Angeles. Mr. Berry self-published his book with an address listed as: 36, Beechfields, Eccleston, Chorley, Lancs., PR7 5RE England.

Accurate mileage accounts on the Bunion Derby are sometimes difficult to obtain. Note that the total daily mileage for that race shown below adds up to 3,371.7 miles. However, when you read accounts of the race, the mileage is generally listed as being about 3,422 miles. Where in the numbers is the 50-mile discrepancy between my daily summaries and the recognized total is anyone's guess.

Perhaps I should have converted the miles into yards like the pamphlet given out at the Andy Payne Memorial Foot Races each year in Oklahoma City. The pamphlet has the headline, "The Great 6,023,248-Yard Dash."

RANDY ELLIS 1998
Mileage

Day	Date	Destination	Day	Total
1	3/28	Santa Clarita, CA	35.0	35.0
2	3/29	Palmdale, CA	33.0	68.0
3	3/30	Victorville, CA	37.0	105.0
4	3/31	Barstow, CA	38.0	143.0
5	4/01	Newberry Spring, CA	36.6	179.6
6	4/02	Bagdad, CA	37.4	217.0
7	4/03	Essex, CA	39.6	256.6
8	4/04	Rt. 66/H-95, CA	34.2	290.8
9	4/05	Near Oatman, AZ	31.0	321.8
10	4/06	Kingman, AZ	38.0	359.8
11	4/07	Truxton, AZ	39.0	398.8
12	4/08	Seligman, AZ	39.8	438.6
13	4/09	Near Williams, AZ	43.4	482.0
14	4/10	Flagstaff, AZ	40.0	522.0
15	4/11	Two Guns, AZ	32.5	554.5
16	4/12	Winslow, AZ	32.0	586.5
17	4/13	Holbrook, AZ	33.0	619.5
18	4/14	Day off	0.0	619.5
19	4/15	Navajo, AZ	37.0	656.5
20	4/16	Lupton, AZ	34.5	691.0
21	4/17	Gallup, NM	31.1	722.1
22	4/18	Prewitt, NM	33.5	755.6
23	4/19	Villa de Cubero, NM	38.5	794.1
24	4/20	Highway 6, NM	37.9	832.0
25	4/21	Highway 47, NM	38.5	870.5
26	4/22	Mountanair, NM	36.0	906.5
27	4/23	Encino, NM	40.3	946.8
28	4/24	Pastura, NM	40.0	986.8
29	4/25	Cuervo, NM	41.0	1027.8
30	4/26	Montoya, NM	20.5	1048.3
31	4/27	Tucumcari, NM	40.0	1088.3
32	4/28	Past Glenrio, TX	38.0	1126.3
33	4/29	Wildorado, TX	40.0	1166.3
34	4/30	Amarillo Exit 85, TX	38.0	1204.3
35	5/01	Exit 124, TX	39.5	1243.8
36	5/02	Shamrock, TX	39.0	1282.8
37	5/03	Sayre, OK	39.0	1321.8
38	5/04	Clinton, OK	39.8	1361.6
39	5/05	Bridgeport, OK	38.0	1399.6

ANDY PAYNE 1928
Mileage

Date	Destination	Day	Total
3/04	Puente, CA	17.0	17.0
3/05	Bloomington,CA	34.7	51.7
3/06	Victorville, CA	45.4	97.1
3/07	Barstow, CA	36.0	133.1
3/08	Mojave Wells,CA	32.5	165.6
3/09	Bagdad, CA	41.9	207.5
3/10	Danby, CA	31.9	239.4
3/11	Needles, CA	57.0	296.4
3/12	Oatman, AZ	20.5	316.9
3/13	Kingman, AZ	28.8	345.7
3/14	Peach Springs,AZ	51.7	397.4
3/15	Seligman, AZ	38.3	435.7
3/16	Williams, AZ	43.9	479.6
3/17	Flagstaff, AZ	36.2	515.8
3/18	Two Guns, AZ	35.8	551.6
3/19	Winslow, AZ	24.1	575.7
3/20	Holbrook, AZ	34.3	610.0
3/21	Navajo, AZ	40.0	650.0
3/22	Lupton, AZ	34.7	684.7
3/23	Gallup, NM	22.8	707.5
3/24	Thoreau, NM	32.8	740.3
3/25	Grants, NM	30.5	770.8
3/26	Laguna, NM	33.9	804.7
3/27	Los Lunas, NM	49.0	853.7
3/28	Seven Springs,NM	37.0	890.7
3/29	Moriarty, NM	29.5	920.2
3/30	Palma, NM	25.0	945.2
3/31	Santa Rosa, NM	45.4	990.6
4/01	Newkirk, NM	32.2	1022.8
4/02	Tucumcari, NM	34.3	1057.1
4/03	Glenrio, TX	44.1	1101.2
4/04	Vega, TX	37.3	1138.5
4/05	Amarillo, TX	37.0	1175.5
4/06	Groom, TX	40.6	1216.1
4/07	McLean, TX	38.8	1254.9
4/08	Texola, TX	35.0	1289.9
4/09	Sayre, OK	32.2	1322.1
4/10	Clinton, OK	50.0	1372.1
4/11	Bridgeport, OK	34.4	1406.5

RANDY ELLIS 1998
Mileage

Day	Date	Destination	Day	Total
40	5/06	Yukon, OK	39.8	1439.4
41	5/07	Arcadia Lake, OK	39.0	1478.4
42	5/08	Davenport, OK	39.5	1517.9
43	5/09	Kellyville, OK	37.0	1554.9
44	5/10	Day off	0.0	1554.9
45	5/11	Sapulpa, OK	13.0	1567.4
46	5/12	Catoosa, OK	35.5	1602.9
47	5/13	Chelsea, OK	36.0	1638.9
48	5/14	Miami, OK	40.7	1679.6
49	5/15	Joplin, MO	36.7	1716.3
50	5/16	Jane, MO	43.0	1759.3
51	5/17	Fayetteville, AR	36.0	1795.3
52	5/18	Mountainburg, AR	41.0	1836.3
53	5/19	Ozark, AR	42.7	1879.0
54	5/20	London, AR	43.7	1922.7
55	5/21	Plumerville, AR	39.6	1962.3
56	5/22	El Paso, AR	37.9	2000.2
57	5/23	Bald Knob, AR	41.5	2041.7
58	5/24	Wynne, AR	41.0	2082.7
59	5/25	Marion, AR	41.5	2124.2
60	5/26	Oakland, TN	45.0	2169.2
61	5/27	Bolivar, TN	35.0	2204.2
62	5/28	Corinth, MS	45.0	2249.2
63	5/29	Barton, AL	39.5	2288.7
64	5/30	Wheeler, AL	43.0	2331.7
65	5/31	Huntsville, AL	42.0	2373.7
66	6/01	Scottsboro, AL	43.3	2417.0
67	6/02	Summerville, GA	43.0	2460.0
68	6/03	Cassville, GA	42.0	2502.0
69	6/04	Ducktown, GA	42.3	2544.3
70	6/05	Russell, GA	44.6	2588.9
71	6/06	Lexington, GA	45.0	2633.9
72	6/07	Lincolnton, GA	43.0	2676.9
73	6/08	Saluda, SC	45.4	2722.3
74	6/09	West Columbia, SC	39.4	2761.7
75	6/10	Sumter, SC	53.0	2814.7
76	6/11	Past Lake City, SC	40.0	2854.7
77	6/12	Conway, SC	42.7	2897.4
78	6/13	Myrtle Beach, SC	16.6	2914.0

ANDY PAYNE 1928
Mileage

Date	Destination	Day	Total
4/12	El Reno, OK	37.0	1443.5
4/13	Oklahoma City	33.0	1476.5
4/14	Chandler, OK	51.9	1528.4
4/15	Bristow, OK	34.8	1563.2
4/16	Tulsa, OK	41.7	1604.9
4/17	Chelsea, OK	50.0	1654.9
4/18	Miami, OK	52.0	1706.9
4/19	Joplin, MO	40.0	1746.9
4/20	Miller, MO	46.7	1793.6
4/21	Springfield, MO	33.6	1827.2
4/22	Conway, MO	43.1	1870.3
4/23	Waynesville, MO	51.9	1922.2
4/24	Rollams, MO	32.4	1954.6
4/25	Sullivan, MO	42.9	1997.5
4/26	Hillside View, MO	45.6	2043.1
4/27	East St. Louis, IL	30.0	2073.1
4/28	Staunton, IL	44.0	2117.1
4/29	Virden, IL	44.0	2161.1
4/30	Springfield, IL	26.0	2187.1
5/01	Lincoln, IL	31.0	2218.1
5/02	Normal, IL	34.0	2252.1
5/03	Pontiac, IL	34.7	2286.8
5/04	Joliet, IL	57.1	2343.9
5/05	Chicago, IL	43.0	2386.9
5/06	Gary, IN	28.4	2415.3
5/07	Mishawaka, IN	66.2	2481.5
5/08	Ligonier, IN	34.0	2515.5
5/09	Butler, IN	41.8	2557.3
5/10	Waseon, OH	44.9	2602.2
5/11	Freemont, OH	60.0	2662.2
5/12	Elyria, OH	63.3	2725.5
5/13	Arrowhead, OH	51.4	2776.9
5/14	Ashtabula, OH	41.1	2818.0
5/15	Erie, PA	45.0	2863.0
5/16	Jamestown, NY	43.0	2906.0
5/17	Bradford, PA	40.0	2946.0
5/18	Wellesville, NY	50.0	2996.0
5/19	Bath, NY	52.0	3048.0
5/20	Waverly, NY	59.0	3107.0

RANDY ELLIS 1998 Mileage				
Day	Date	Destination	Day	Total

ANDY PAYNE 1928 Mileage			
Date	Destination	Day	Total
5/21	Deposit, NY	73.0	3180.0
5/22	Liberty, NY	57.0	3237.0
5/23	Middleton, NY	38.0	3275.0
5/24	Suffern, NY	36.0	3311.0
5/25	Passaic, NJ	24.0	3335.0
5/26	New York, NY	36.7	3371.7

*Down the wooden steps, heading for the water
at Myrtle Beach State Park.*

172

COMPARISON OF THE TWO ROUTES

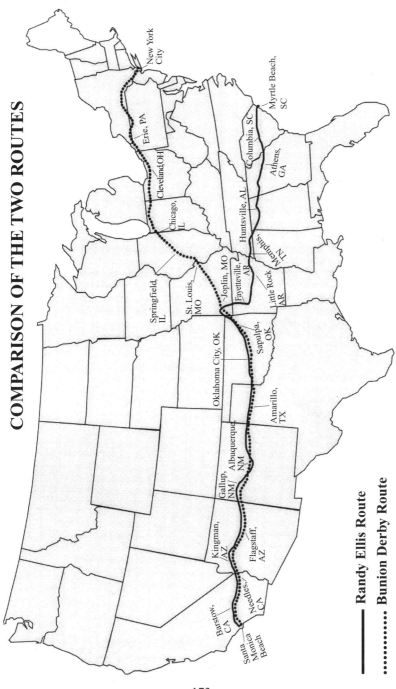

New York City

Erie, PA

Cleveland, OH

Chicago, IL

Myrtle Beach, SC

Columbia, SC

Athens, GA

Huntsville, AL

Memphis, TN

Springfield, IL

St. Louis, MO

Joplin, MO

Fayetteville, AR

Little Rock, AR

Oklahoma City, OK

Sapulpa, OK

Amarillo, TX

Albuquerque, NM

Gallup, NM

Kingman, AZ

Flagstaff, AZ

Barstow, CA

Needles, CA

Santa Monica Beach

—— Randy Ellis Route

••••••• Bunion Derby Route

Appendix II

THE TOP TEN QUESTIONS

IN THE MONTHS and years after my coast-to-coast run, I enjoyed answering people's questions. Eventually, I could anticipate the most frequently asked questions. Here are the top ten questions and my answers:

10. What about your job?

I left my job as controller of Parker Drilling Company about two months before I started my run. The most frequent unstated question was, "What kind of an idiot would leave a good job to run across the country?" Answer: there's only one person that I have ever heard of doing that.

After the run, I worked one school year as Maggie Bennett's 4th grade assistant teacher at Pretty Water School (the actual name of the school). Two years before the run, I had been president of the Pretty Water School Board. In two years, I had gone from president to teacher's assistant.

After a school year of lots of fun, but little pay, I returned to the business world as controller of CCI Corporation. The CCI Corporation folks (and others) have often wondered why they hired a guy crazy enough to run across the country.

9. Did you ever hitch a ride?

What kind of a fool would I have been to go to all that trouble and then not run every step of the way? No rides! I covered all the miles on foot. The long-time dream wasn't about running and riding across the country; it was about running across the country.

8. Did anyone run with you?
Yes, but for only a total of about 150 miles of the 2,914 miles. My dad occasionally ran with me early in the journey, and several friends joined me in various places across Oklahoma. Of course, the best part was my family running with me the last mile through Myrtle Beach State Park.

7. Did you have any injuries?
I don't count the normal and expected aches, pains, and blisters as injuries. I only had two significant problems, including a severe shin splint for several days in Arizona and a pulled Achilles tendon for a few days in New Mexico. I attribute to God's grace the fact that the two injuries went away and I had no more problems than that.

6. Where did you sleep?
Before the run, I bought an older 26-foot motor home. My dad was generally the chauffeur. The motor home served as living and sleeping quarters for all but nine nights.

We parked in many campgrounds across the United States; however, there were many nights where campgrounds were not available. The non-campground places ranged from the middle of the desert to a grocery store parking lot.

5. What did you eat?
Food had to qualify in two ways: edible and available. A ravaging appetite is not a discriminating appetite. Pasta, bread, and fruit were generally a part of the evening meal. No Atkins diet here. You diet purists cover your eyes — I also consumed many desserts and soft drinks. Edible and available, I tell you, those were the only requirements.

4. Did someone follow you?

Dad would generally let me run a few miles up the road and then catch up in the motor home for a short break. At other times, he would drive ahead anywhere from three to six miles and wait for me to catch up to him.

3. How did you train for the run?

Logging many miles of running and walking, lifting light weights, and doing many sit-ups. I steadily increased my weekly mileage and did several weeks of 100 to 120 miles. During the last six weeks, training seemed to take as much time as a full-time job — the full-time job that I no longer had.

2. How many pair of shoes did you use?

I bought six new pair of Asics shoes and lightly broke them in before I started. I numbered the shoes with a magic marker so that I could rotate the shoes, using a different pair each day. Later I ordered four new pair and rotated them. (Though I rotated, I didn't balance them. Remember, it wasn't the shoes that were out of balance.) Each of the ten pair had nearly 300 miles on them by journey's end. Most of the shoes are in a box in the attic, probably making a good home for the mice.

1. Why?

I've attempted to answer this question many times, including in the first chapter of this book. Some questions just never seem to have a satisfying answer.

Appendix III

PEOPLE WHO SENT E-MAILS DURING THE RUN

Affleck, Marge
Andrews, Eva
Andrews, Tom
Ashworth, Harry and Ferris Ann
Baker, Michelle Reed
Bartholomew, Bob and Barbara
Baskin, Joani
Beard, Caryl
Bell, Audra
Bell, Tommy
Bennett, Mrs. — 4th Grade Class
Beverlin, Dave
Bishop, John
Blackburn, Sam and Monica
Blackwell, Jeff
Blackwell, Randy and Lynna
Blewitt, Earl
Bonino, Jan
Boyd, Mary
Bradley, Bob and Ann
Bradley, Don and Deena
Brannin, Graham
Brewer, Mark
Briggs, Tom
Brim, Janice
Browning, Tara
Burch, Phil
Burcham, Ryan
Busch, Bonnie
Caloway, Curt
Chapman, Richard
Cherry, Charles
Childress, George and Linda
Choisnet, Barbara
Christian, Jack and Brenda
Colwell, Tim
Cooper, Judy
Corter, Sandra
Craft, Wanda
Crawford, Jerry
Currier, Aaron
d'Avignon, Jodee

Dancer, Jackie
Davidson, Janice
Davis, Jim
Davis, John
Davis, John and Martha
Dawson, Terry and Portia
Deupree, Harry
Dice, Fred
Eidel, Charlie
Elliott, Russ
Ellis, Craig, Mindy, Sam, and Ben
Ellis, Doug
Ellis, Jewell
Ellis, Jim
Ellis, Marcy, Heather, Justin, and Nicole
Ellis, Marvin and Shirley
Ellis, Wayne, Cindy, Daniel, Ryan, Nathan, Brandon, Kaitlynn
Esau, Michelle
Faith Christian Academy (Libby Stephens)
Fanning, Mike
Ferguson, John
Fox, Roger
Frederick, Alma
Freeman, Corey
Freeman, Eric, Laurie, Joel, Darby, Dustin, Jessica
Galbraith, Pete
Gent, Jimmy
Godale, Mark
Gomoljack, Jenny and Dick
Gordon, Lee
Graham, Dick
Greydanus, John
Grundy, Sylvia
Hall, Linda and Larry
Hammerschmitt, Leland
Hardee, Randy, Glenna, Randy Jr., Josh, Brandon
Harrison, Steve
Harvey, Jim and Jewell
Hathaway, Mark and Billie

Hawkins, Jane
Hawley, Kent
Haynes, Bill
Heck, Doug
Helsel, Richard
Henderson, Carl, Lynn, Brady, Blake
Herring, Cathy
Herring, Layne
Hill, Steve, Peggy, Kelly
Hinton, Claude
Hipsher, Terry
Hoit, Ken
Horner, Steve
Hughes, Dick and Freida
Hyslop, Philo, Tara, Jenna, Jessica
Jeffries, Mike and David
Johnson, Wally
Jones, Doug and Debbie
Jones, Geoff
Karasek, Tanya
Knam, Michael
Korver, Bruce
Lafreniere, Pierre
Landrum, Hilary and Terry
Langley, Ted
Laurence, Sheila
Lemaire, Mark
Lewis, Gary
Lindley, Judy
Linn, Jim
Linthicum, Lisa
Long, Steve
Love, Thomas
Lovelace, Neil
LSU Greek Affairs Staff
Loy, Sam
Maddy, Robert
Makela, Michelle
Malone, Megan
Marker, Cathy
Mauch, Fred
McBride, Daryl
McClendon, Jennie
McClung, Captain Joe
McClung, Lynn
McDaniel, Joe
McDonald, Susan

McGillivray, Dave
McIntyre, James
McKenzie, Ronnie
McPhail, Mark
Mikolic, Karen
Milroy, Andy
Mollock, Jerry
Neil, Jerry and Sue
Nelsen, John
Olds, Cathy
O'Neil, Merilee
Parker, Bobby and Risa
Parker, Doug
Peoples, Rhonda
Peters, Todd
Pierre, Holly Neil
Pinkstaff, Sandy and George
Platner, Eric and Carrie
Platner, Prince and Marty
Pollard, Greg and Kathy
Pontius, Dionna
Pretty Water 4th and 7th grades
Pritz, David, Marsha, Scott, Emily, Ted
Pritz, Gordon
Pritz, Ray and Eileen
Pryor, Antwine and Delores
Queen, Dennis
Rector, Jack and Sherri
Reed, Marshall
Roark, Scott
Roberts, Tim
Robertson, Mark
Robertson, Matt
Rosencutter, Sue
Sanders, Susan
Sandoval, V.
Schultz, Bill
Seals, Patrick
Skidmore, George
Skinner, Lloyd and Sue
Slockers, Caroline and Erik
Smith, Jeff, Lila, Sarah, Keith
Smith, Rod
Smith, Shannon and Robin
Spanz, Siegfried
Spencer, Donna and David
Stasso, Paul and Vicki

Steele, Janet
Stewart, Michael
Stone, Rocky, Brenda, Ryan, Amber
Storjohann, David, Cindy, Josh, Steven,
    Rachel
Sullivan, Chuck
Sweet, Janice
Swift, Ed
Taylor, Craig
Taylor, Doug
Taylor, Randy
Thomas, Andrew
Thomas, Ed and Carol
Thomas, Philip
Thompson, Brent
Thornton, Iris
Tockner, Franz

Tracy, John
Truelove, Emilee
Truelove, Burf and Terri Sue
Tucker, David
Vance, Jay and Lina
Vaughan, David
Vineyard, Jim
Vinson, John
Walters, Mary
Watson, Rick
Weekley, Josh
White, Jim and Rochelle
White, Rick, Lori, Megan, Matthew
Williams, Wayne
Wing, Jack and Sharon
Wood, John

PEOPLE WHO COMMITTED TO PRAY DURING THE RUN

Ashworth, Harry and Ferris Ann
Basinger, Trula
Boyd, Avery and Mary
Buchanan, Chuck and My
Cotner, Ed and Rose
Cross, Phil and Pat
Dawson, Terry and Portia
Echols, Francis
Ellis, Betty
Ellis, Craig and Mindy
Ellis, Justin
Ellis, Marvin and Shirley
Ellis, Nicole
Ellis, Sam
Ellis, Wayne, Cyndy, Nathan
Emmons, Matt and Carol
Emmons, Roy and Norma
Freeman, Eric and Laurie
Harvey, Jim and Jewell
Heck, Doug
Hill, Judy and family
Hughes, Freida and Dick

Johnson, Jo
Johnson, John
Jordan, Joe and Denise
Karasek, John and Tanya
King, Kevin and Laurie
Long, Dulcie
Mix, Larry and Judy
Monger, Pat
Neil, Sue
Nichols, Marian
Ondracek, Laddie and Mary
Painter, Lisa and family
Platner, Marty
Pritz, Dave, Marsha, and family
Pritz, Ray and Eileen
Smith, Betty
Smith, Janis
Swift, Phyllis
Thomas, Roger and Janet
Vernon, Barbara and Bob
Walters, Mary and Ken
Whiteside, Myldred

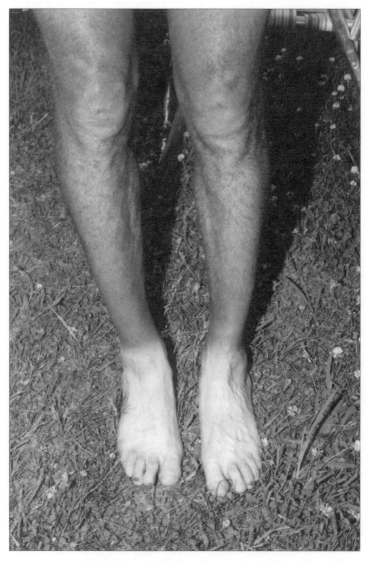

Note the very dark legs and the very white feet!

To order additional books or for more information,
please visit our website:

www.runningwithpayne.com